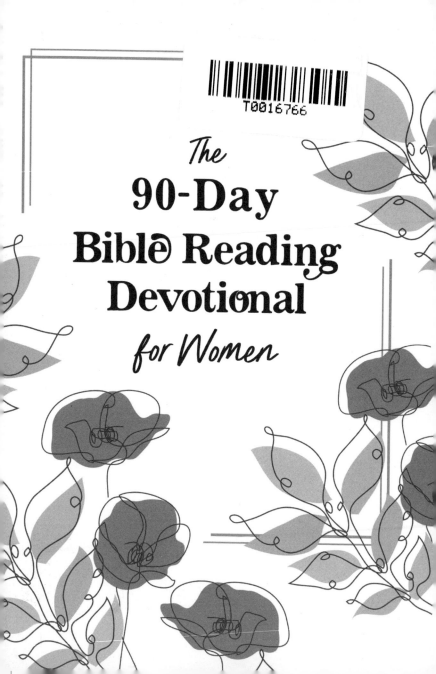

The
90-Day
Bible Reading
Devotional
for Women

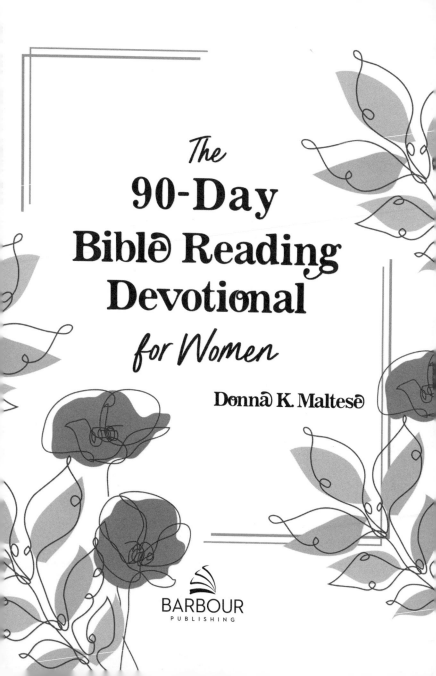

The
90-Day
Bible Reading
Devotional

for Women

Donna K. Maltese

BARBOUR

PUBLISHING

Introduction

God is speaking to all of us, all the time. The question is not, to whom does God talk? The question is, who listens?

NEALE DONALD WALSH, AUTHOR

Welcome to *The 90-Day Bible Reading Devotional for Women*, a place where you can commune with God, His Word, and the Holy Spirit. This is your entrance into a quiet time of prayer, reading, and reflection, a way of discovering what God is speaking into your life and what He is saying to you and you alone so that you know where to go, what to do, how to think, what to say.

The 90-Day Bible Reading Devotional for Women contains three topical 30-day Bible reading plans to help you focus on the following areas:

- Getting to Know God Better (pages 7–67)
- Knowing Jesus Better (pages 69–129)
- Growing in Your Faith (pages 131–191)

Each of the 90 days contains that day's specific topic, scripture reading, and two to three questions to contemplate after you've completed your scripture reading for that day.

Before beginning each day's Bible passage, *pray* for the Holy Spirit's illumination. Make it your intention to *listen* to what God is saying. Then and only then, *absorb* the Bible passage for that day. Afterward, before looking at any commentary or considering that day's questions, *mark* the verse or passage that is specifically speaking to your heart in this place and time—whether or not you understand why. Then go on to the questions for that day. Slowly *reflect* upon each one. *Consider* the question that most speaks to you—or the verse you have already marked—and see what more God may reveal. The point is to follow where God is leading. At the end of your reflection time, read the devotional and pray the prayer that follows. As you pray, remember to ask God to embellish in your own heart, soul, and life the truths He has imparted and for His strength and courage to go where the signpost has pointed.

Within these pages is your opportunity to take hold of your God, voice, thoughts, purpose, dreams, spirit, and life. And trust you will find the path, the clue, the word to be followed.

Everything in the Scriptures is God's Word. All of it is useful for teaching and helping people and for correcting them and showing them how to live.

2 TIMOTHY 3:16 CEV

30 Days of Bible Readings for Getting to Know God Better

*This is what the LORD says. . . "Those who wish
to boast should boast in this alone: that they
truly know me and understand that I am the
LORD who demonstrates unfailing love."*

JEREMIAH 9:23–24 NLT

God is the author of the Bible, a love letter from His heart to yours. And from Genesis to Revelation, He clearly makes it known who He is and what role He will take in every area and aspect of your life.

In this first of three 30-day Bible reading plans, you will be exploring scriptures to better understand God's majesty, power, and love for you. It begins with God the Creator and ends with God the Approachable.

As you enter into your Bible reading each day, start off with a simple prayer, something like "Here I am, Lord. Speak, for Your servant is listening. I'm determined to hear what You want to tell me, to learn what You want me to know." Then read that day's scripture, intending to hear God's voice. Meditate upon it. Then, and only then, expecting God to reveal Himself, read and reflect upon the questions from that day's reading, being honest with yourself and God. Afterward, read that day's devotion and pray, thanking God for this time together, asking Him to help you apply what you've learned to your life and heart and to follow where He is leading.

Day 1
God the Creator

Read Genesis 1:1–2:3

In the beginning God created the heaven and the earth. And the earth was without form, and void; and darkness was upon the face of the deep. And the Spirit of God moved upon the face of the waters.

GENESIS 1:1–2 KJV

- The Spirit of God hovers over the darkness (Genesis 1:2), the unknown, looking to create order. How might this bring you comfort?

- What God speaks comes into being, is created. What are you speaking? What is being created in your life?

- What does it mean to you that you have been created in the image of God, that He has blessed you, wants you to be fruitful, provides for you, and believes you are very good?

After God had created everything, He took some time to look it over, "savoring its beauty and appreciating its goodness" (Genesis 1:31 VOICE).

Like God, in whose image we've been made, we too are designed to create beauty, to do what we can to bring goodness into this world. But how often do we take the time to look over what we have done—not to take pride in our accomplishments but to lift them up to God for His blessing and approval? Do we take time to savor how nice the bulbs we planted in the fall look when they bloom in the spring? To appreciate the goodness we see in the face of a child who is learning to walk? To thank God for the talents He has given us to shape the words we write, the designs we draw, the food we cook, the child we raise, the songs we sing?

Look around today at what you have helped to birth or create. Take some time to enjoy its splendor, to lift it up to God for His blessing and appreciation. Take a moment to delight in the goodness you have unleashed into the world. Savor this moment.

Thank You, God the Creator, for making me in Your image. May I follow Your example by bringing beauty and goodness into this world and then taking time to savor the moment.

9

Day 2
God the Sustainer

Read Genesis 2:4–24

*Then God planted a garden in Eden, in the east.
He put the Man he had just made in it. God
made all kinds of trees grow from the ground,
trees beautiful to look at and good to eat.*

Genesis 2:8–9 msg

- To *sustain* means to support, continue to hold up without fail. How does it feel knowing God has created all things to hold you up—including the earth beneath your feet—and continues to do so in your life today?

- God formed the earthly body of Adam (meaning *earth*) from the soil but formed Eve (meaning *life*), his equal partner, not from the earth or the animal kingdom but from the rib of man himself. What does this tell you about God as a *creative* sustainer?

When God realized Adam needed a helper, one who would not only be a companion to him but a proper partner to help him tend the garden, He formed a creature of Adam's ilk. Adam, who readily and gladly accepted this new being, named his friend "woman." This act of God proves He is prescient, knowing what His children need before they do and then meeting that need.

Let this be a reminder that God has been taking care of you from the very beginning of time. He planted you in the womb from which you were birthed into being. He gave you your body, spirit, and soul. He supplied you with His breath of life. He tended to you as you suckled, crawled, toddled, walked, and then ran. And He will continue to supply what you need before you need it.

Take that truth to heart. Plant it deep within your mind and soul. Accept that there is never ever anything for you to worry about—because God the Sustainer will continually meet your need. Allow this truth to give you calm and comfort today and every day.

Thank You, God the Sustainer, for always supporting me. Thank You for this beautiful garden called Earth, the air I breathe, the food I eat, and the water I drink. Because You are and always will be here to take care of me, I need neither fear nor fret. Amen.

Day 3
God of Promises

Read Genesis 15

*One day, the word of the Eternal One came to Abram
through a vision—a kind of waking dream.*
Eternal One: *Do not be afraid, Abram. I am
always your shield and protector. Your reward
for loyalty and trust will be immense.*

GENESIS 15:1 VOICE

- God talked to Abram in a vision. In what ways is He talking to you?

- God told Abram not to fear before the man even confessed he was worried and had nothing *but* questions. How does this scenario comfort you?

- On one side are God's promises that reach beyond time and space. On the other, your trust and reliance on them. Which of God's promises is He relaying to you, waiting for you to trust Him for, today?

Fears can drive us to panic. That's why God wants us to continually look to His promises. They are His reassurance that no matter how things may seem or appear, He has a better plan, a bigger plan, as He continually works to shield us from harm.

Yet there's one catch: to gain the assurance of God's promises, to rid ourselves of fears, we must have faith that God will always shield and protect us; that in the end, because of our trust in Him, we will be rewarded.

It was faith that prompted Abraham to travel to an unknown land, not even knowing where God was leading him, nor worrying about what he might find along the way. When God spoke His promises, "he [Abram] believed in (trusted in, relied on, remained steadfast to) the Lord, and He counted it to him as righteousness (right standing with God)" (Genesis 15:6 AMPC).

Tonight, allow God to take you outside of yourself. Follow His prompting to look up toward the heavens and count the stars. Know that God's power and promises are limitless, just like the stars in the sky. Allow His truths, words, and actions to prompt you to a limitless faith.

Lord of my heart and life, help me grow my faith so that it will be as limitless as Your power and promises.

Day 4
God of Holiness

Read Exodus 3

GOD saw that he had stopped to look. God called to him from out of the bush, "Moses! Moses!" He said, "Yes? I'm right here!" God said, "Don't come any closer. Remove your sandals from your feet. You're standing on holy ground."

EXODUS 3:4–5 MSG

- When was the last time you "took off your sandals" when meeting with God to show respect and reverence for His holiness?

- In what ways do you pause in God's presence, preparing yourself—mind, body, heart, spirit, and soul—for a heavenly meeting, knowing you, the imperfect being, are approaching the perfect being?

- How does your acknowledgment of God's holiness affect you—before, during, and after prayer?

Moses' encounter with God began on an ordinary day. He was out doing his usual job, shepherding his father-in-law Jethro's flock of sheep. But for some reason, Moses "guided the flock far away from its usual pastures to the other side of the desert and came to a place known as Horeb, where the mountain of God stood" (Exodus 3:1 VOICE). It was in this place that Moses noticed a bush that continued to burn and, curious, turned from the path he was going to take so that he could get a closer look.

You too can meet with God on any ordinary day, a day in which you're doing the usual thing. But to see Him up close, you must follow the leading of your spirit, go where it beckons you go. And you must be curious to get a closer look at your Holy God.

Today, take that turn out of your usual way. Follow your spirit to where God would have you be. Allow your curiosity to get a closer view. Then, as God sees you stop, He will call out to you. He will tell you what to do as you enter into His presence, where the imperfect spirit of woman meets the perfect Spirit of God.

I yearn to come closer to You, God. Lead my spirit where You would have me go. And may my curiosity lead me into Your presence, my imperfect spirit humbled before Your perfection.

Day 5
God the Victor

Read Exodus 15:1–21

"I will sing to the LORD, for he has triumphed gloriously. . . .
The LORD is my strength and my song; he has given me
victory. This is my God, and I will praise him. . . . With
your unfailing love you lead the people you have redeemed.
In your might, you guide them to your sacred home."
EXODUS 15:1–2, 13 NLT

- After miraculously escaping the Egyptian pharaoh and his army, God's people sang a song of victory, saying God, their strength and their song, had become their salvation. On what occasion(s) have you come out of a battle unscathed and sung a victory song to the Lord?

- What do you need to do today to tap into God's strength, assured that with Him you need fear no enemy or flood, and will, in the end, find firm footing on dry land?

You are a valued daughter of God, a princess of a Holy King. Because you follow Him without question, He will always be there for you. Nothing can come against you that He cannot overpower with His love and strength. You can always count on your Lord to step in to fight for you, regardless of how impossible to win the battles appear. By His grace, He will work to save you over and over again.

Today, tap into the strength of that truth. Realize that just as God worked a miracle with the Israelites, He can and will do so for you. For just when they were at a dead end, with no imaginable hope of escape, God did the unimaginable. He saved their lives and souls and demolished their enemies.

In this life, do your part in this walk with God and allow Him to do His, confident that He is ready, willing, and able to bring you to victory, no matter what your particular battle or foe.

Thank You, Lord, for being my strength, my defender, my song, my Savior. No matter what battle I face, I am certain You can lead me to victory. Thus, I need not fear. I can walk in confidence knowing You are by my side, able to protect me from whatever danger comes my way.

Day 6
God of Purity

Read Exodus 20

Then God began to speak directly to all the people. . . .
I am the Eternal your God. I led you out of Egypt
and liberated you from lives of slavery and oppression.
You are not to serve any other gods before Me.

EXODUS 20:1–3 VOICE

- Why do you think God wrote these Ten Commandments, which clearly point out God's purity and human-kind's impurity?

- The first four commandments are about your relationship with God, and the rest are about your relationship with others. Where might you be falling short?

- What might God be pointing out to you in today's reading? What do you need to confess to draw nearer to Him?

God is all good. Pure. There is nothing in Him of evil or corruptness. He is a perfect God of light, love, mercy, grace, and forgiveness. And then there's us. We have our faults, our dark sides. We sometimes have trouble loving others, extending to them mercy and grace. And forgiveness is a hurdle in many situations.

To help us find our way, God gave us the Ten Commandments. When we couldn't keep to those rules, He gave us Jesus. And Jesus boiled down all Ten Commandments to two: love God with all your heart, soul, and mind, and love others as yourself (Matthew 22:36-40). That's all we are to do. If we follow those directives, we'll meet all the requirements of the Ten Commandments.

Today, ask God to help you become more like Him. You've already come so far. He can help you the rest of the way. And if you stumble, know that He will not leave you lying there but will pull you up by His hand. He will listen to anything you may need to confess. He will give you the strength to do all you need to do and get to where He would have you be.

Lord, help me make my connection with You, others, and myself all about love. Help me eschew the darkness and grow ever closer to Your light.

Day 7
God of Glory

Read Exodus 33:7–23

Behold, there is a place beside Me, and you shall stand upon the rock, and while My glory passes by, I will put you in a cleft of the rock and cover you with My hand until I have passed by. Then I will take away My hand and you shall see My back; but My face shall not be seen.

EXODUS 33:21–23 AMPC

- Moses asked to see God's glory but could not see God's face and live. So God protected Moses by putting him in a cleft of rock and covering him with His hand as He went by. This allowed Moses to see God's back but not His face. What does this tell you of the love and care of God for His people?

- In what ways do you experience God's glory in nature? In the rest of God's creation? In your life?

Moses yearned to see more of his Lord, to know more about Him, to experience God's presence in a more personal way. Yet God told him that no human can see His face and live. So to protect Moses' life and yet honor his request, God arranged things so that Moses could see the glory of His presence by covering His servant with His hand until after He had passed by.

Sometimes we ask God for things that are not safe for us to see or have. Yet He unstintingly provides what we can handle. Even to this day, God provides for us, showing us His glory in a sunset, a mountaintop, a spouting whale—all the goodness He has to offer.

Today, ask God to show you His glory, His presence, through His goodness, His mercy, His magnificent creation. Keep your own eyes open for God's glory, knowing He will keep you safe as you get your fill of your Lord, Master, Creator, Provider, and Mercy Giver and all you need to serve Him.

Open my eyes to Your presence in my life today, Lord. Show me Your glory, the beauty of Your creation, the wonder of Your company. Your doing so will revive my passion to serve and follow You, in this life and the next.

Day 8
God of Blessing

Read Deuteronomy 28

Moses: *If you listen closely to the voice of the Eternal your God and carefully obey all the commands I'm giving you today, He'll lift you up high above every other nation on earth. All of the following blessings will be yours—in fact, they'll chase after you—if you'll listen to what He tells you.*

DEUTERONOMY 28:1–2 VOICE

- God says that if you listen to and obey His voice, a myriad of blessings will come down upon you and overtake you. When have you felt God's blessings do just that as a result of your listening to His voice?

- God wants you to continue following His path, not turn aside to go another way. What spiritual practice have you found that keeps you in His way? How well are you keeping to that practice? What blessings do you lose when you stray from His way?

Your actions, the thoughts you think, and the words you say all have consequences in this life. To keep us safe and on the right track, God has set up some parameters for us so that we won't crash and burn. And if we abide by His constraints,

He'll reward us in a very active way. For He doesn't just say we'll be blessed but that His blessings *will chase after us*!

Stop for a moment and imagine a blessing chasing after you. Imagine being content, well provided for, and prosperous. See yourself being "blessed when you go out of your home and blessed when you return to your home" (Deuteronomy 28:6 VOICE). Imagine God defeating your enemies, blessing all you do, and giving "you more than enough of every good thing" (Deuteronomy 28:11 VOICE)—all because you obey His commands, walk His way, and stay upon His path, the one He has created especially for you.

Today, consider what path you have been walking and the results of that route. Then ask God to help you make whatever changes are necessary so that His blessings will begin or continue to chase you down.

Help me, Lord, not to deviate from the path that You have set out for me. Help me make whatever corrections are needed so that my desires align with Yours and Your blessings chase me down.

Day 9
God of Judgment

Read Judges 10:6–16

The People of Israel said to GOD: "We've sinned. Do to us whatever you think best, but please, get us out of this!" Then they cleaned house of the foreign gods and worshiped only GOD. And GOD took Israel's troubles to heart.

JUDGES 10:15–16 MSG

- In what ways do you at times forsake God, worshipping other things and people instead of Him?

- When was the last time you—having done other than God desired and feeling His judgment because of it—cried out for help?

- How, in His mercy and compassion, has God rescued you from yourself? In what ways do you think your troubles became His? How does this view—that what hurts you hurts God—change your perception of Him?

When times are light and easy, people tend to drift away from God. They begin to believe they really no longer need Him. After all, they can take care of themselves, right? Before they know it, they've stopped reading His Word, praying through His Spirit, and doing what Jesus would do.

Once people believe themselves self-sufficient, they soon find things going from good to not-so-good to quite awful. They, like the prodigal son, then have a moment when they come to their senses. They realize how far they've moved away from God. They look around and begin to ask themselves, "What am I doing here?" (Luke 15:17 VOICE). Finally, the drifters come up with a plan: "I'll get up and return to my father, and I'll say, 'Father, I have done wrong—wrong against God and against you'" (Luke 15:18 VOICE).

Fortunately for wanderers, God is only too happy to see them return to the fold. He opens His arms of compassion and welcomes them home (Luke 15:20), taking their "troubles to heart."

Where do you rank on the wandering-prodigal scale? Maybe it's time to come to your senses and check in with God once more.

Lord, forgive me for wandering out of Your way, for hurting You as well as myself. Pour Your compassion out upon me as I run into Your arms. Take my troubles to heart once more.

Day 10
God the Unrivaled

Read 1 Kings 18:16–46

Immediately the fire of GOD fell and burned up the offering, the wood, the stones, the dirt, and even the water in the trench. All the people saw it happen and fell on their faces in awed worship, exclaiming, "GOD is the true God! GOD is the true God!"

1 KINGS 18:38–39 MSG

- What false god may be rivaling for your allegiance in your own life? What might you need to do to rebuild your altar to the Lord?

- God—the one who has power over fire, water, clouds, and rain—desires the entire heart, mind, body, soul, and spirit of His people. What can you do to show Him you are wholly His?

- How does it feel knowing you are the daughter of an unrivaled God?

In the Old and New Testaments, God proves over and over again that He is superior to all other gods that we might encounter. He's more powerful than the almighty dollar. He can outdo any pagan god you can dream of. Your God can part mighty seas, stop the sun in the sky, and rain down fire and brimstone. He can turn a man in hiding into one of the greatest judges, make a way for an elderly couple to bear a child, and raise people from the dead.

All this unrivaled God asks of you is to believe in Him and love Him, to love others and yourself. He urges you to, like Elijah, tap into the power of prayer. For then you can change not just the weather (1 Kings 18:41–46) but the world and the people in it!

Today, go to your God of victory. Get down on your knees; fall on your face in worship. Let Him know He is the true God of your heart and home. Then ask Him to walk with you, to help you fight any evil that has come against you, to help you overcome whatever obstacle is facing you. Know that He will answer your prayers for you. He "can do anything, you know—far more than you could ever imagine or guess or request in your wildest dreams!" (Ephesians 3:20 MSG).

Lord unrivaled, I am wholly Yours. My entire being bows to You. How may I serve You—and You alone?

Day 11
God of Majesty

Read Psalm 8

When I view and consider Your heavens, the work of Your fingers, the moon and the stars, which You have ordained and established, what is man that You are mindful of him, and the son of [earthborn] man that You care for him?

PSALM 8:3–4 AMPC

- When was the last time you stopped and truly considered the majesty of God, the awesome works of His creation that surround you every day?

- What range of emotions do you feel knowing that although you are just a speck in God's universe, you are also His beloved daughter, a crowned princess?

- What things has God put into your hands and under your feet? How is His majesty reflected in these things, large and small?

We can see God reflected in everything that surrounds us, if only we'd take the time to look up from our books, cell phones, TVs, and computer screens. If we'd take a break from all the things that distract us from God's presence, we might see His hand more in our lives and the lives of those around us.

God doesn't want His believers to be so tuned in to this world that we tune out His. This will take some effort on our part, as do all good things. This may mean taking a walk each day, giving yourself a chance to realize all the good that He has created around you but that you've been taking for granted. It may mean getting up early to see the sunrise or reaching down to pick up a pretty seashell, a brightly colored leaf, or a unique stone. It may mean walking away from the computer screen so that you can catch the sun as it sinks below the horizon. It may mean missing your favorite show so that you can get to know the constellations in the sky.

Where will you see God's majesty today? What might you do to protect it?

Open my eyes to Your majesty that surrounds me,
Lord. What needs my care? In what may
I see Your splendor reflected?

Day 12
God of Life

Read Psalm 16

I will bless the Lord, Who has given me counsel; yes, my heart instructs me in the night seasons. I have set the Lord continually before me; because He is at my right hand, I shall not be moved. Therefore my heart is glad and my glory [my inner self] rejoices; my body too shall rest and confidently dwell in safety.

PSALM 16:7–9 AMPC

- What words is your soul speaking to the Lord today?

- When was the last time you asked God for advice; allowed Him to speak to your heart in the night; set Him at your right hand, knowing that with Him there you need not worry about anything because He is your protector in your life journey?

- In what ways have you allowed God to show you the path of life and, in so doing, found joy in His presence and pleasure in eternal life with Him?

Your God is not some mighty being that stands far off and aloof, unable to hear, see, smell, taste, or touch you. No. Your God is something and someone else. He is a personal partner in your life story. In fact, He's already authored your story. He knows what's going to happen from beginning to end. He knows all the plot twists and turns. And if there is anyone or anything that can help you navigate your way through this life on earth, it's God.

Psalm 16, written by King David, reminds us of the best course we can take as we continue in our journey. Just reading through it reminds us that God is our safe harbor when we make it a practice to seek Him. That He is the only source of good in this world, the one who holds our future in His hands. That all we have, all our blessings, come from His hand. That He is one who will never desert us.

Today and tonight, open up your heart, mind, and soul to God. Allow Him to speak to your spirit. Know that with Him, you are in the safest hands—on earth and in heaven.

Thank You, Lord, for being so near and dear to me. I come to You, seeking warmth, love, safety, and good advice. Lead on, Lord. Lead on.

Day 13
God of Supremacy

Read Psalm 19

The heavens proclaim the glory of God. The skies display his craftsmanship. Day after day they continue to speak; night after night they make him known. They speak without a sound or word; their voice is never heard. Yet their message has gone throughout the earth, and their words to all the world.

PSALM 19:1–4 NLT

- What have you witnessed in God's creation that tells you of His overwhelming supremacy over all of nature?

- In what ways does God reveal Himself and His power in your soul, thoughts, heart, and spirit?

- In what ways have you not given God free "reign" in your life, so that your words, actions, thoughts, heart, soul, and spirit will be pleasing to Him, the ruler of all?

Just by looking up at the sky, you can see God's handiwork on display. For it is He who spoke the world into being. He was the artist who designed and crafted not just our planet but the entire universe. The sunrise, the sunset, the darkness of the night sky lit by the stars and planets leave us in awe.

They cannot speak, but their very presence declares God's supremacy. And He runs this world like clockwork.

Yet we often have this notion that although it's clear that the Lord reigns over nature, we can take the reins of our own lives and probably do just as well as He. But this is a fallacy. And usually leads us into trouble.

If God is the copilot in your life, it'd be best for you to let Him take the wheel. For He alone can see the future. He knows what you've left behind and where you are in this moment. He sees the entire picture, devised the plan, and knows your place in it. And if you are wise, you'll give Him free reign so that you will please the God who is supreme.

Lord, I give myself wholly to You. Take over the reins of my life. For when You do, I know I'll be in the best possible hands.

Day 14
God the Shepherd

Read Psalm 23

The Lord is my Shepherd [to feed, guide, and shield me], I shall not lack. He makes me lie down in [fresh, tender] green pastures; He leads me beside the still and restful waters.
PSALM 23:1–2 AMPC

- As you imagine God as your Shepherd—the one who provides for you, gives you rest, stills your spirit, restores your soul, comforts you, guards you, and guides you—which of His provisions speaks to you the most today? Why?

- What dark valley might you be walking through right now? What light is God shining into it?

- How would your life change if you were conscious every moment that God the Shepherd is walking with you, leading you, has got you covered?

Sometimes our worries can lead us to fear and insecurities, ones that may be hard to shake. But God wants us to know that we need not be concerned about anything. For each of us is a sheep in His rich pasture. And He continually invites us to follow Him to fresh green pastures and still, peaceful waters.

No matter what comes your way, God will be there for you, ready to lead you to rest, provision, and security. Even in your darkest moments, you can know that He's there with you to protect and guide you. You cannot shake Him off.

Today and every day, before your feet hit the floor, remember who is with you, leading you, comforting you, protecting you. Know that He will continually replenish and revive you with His presence. With the Lord God your Shepherd actively participating in your life, you will never lack. *Never!* In fact, about Him you can say, "Certainly Your faithful protection and loving provision will pursue me where I go, always, everywhere. I will always be with the Eternal, in Your house forever" (Psalm 23:6 VOICE). Dear woman, it doesn't get any better than that!

With You in my life, Good Shepherd, I am
safe, secure, protected, provided for, and
loved, lacking absolutely nothing.

Day 15
God of Peace

Read Psalm 29

*Above the floodwaters is GOD's throne from which
his power flows, from which he rules the world. GOD
makes his people strong. GOD gives his people peace.*
PSALM 29:10–11 MSG

- In what ways do you praise and worship God before, during, and after the storms in your life? How might worshipping God *before* the storm help you endure it, to find peace amid the thunder and lightning?

- What comfort does it give you knowing God is more powerful than any storm you could encounter or witness, that even in the deluge, He is still on the throne and always will be?

- Where and in what situation are you craving God's strength and peace?

No matter what storms we may encounter, God is with us. He is the one constant in our lives, the one thing that never changes. And although His voice at times roars like thunder, exploding in great power over planet Earth, He is also the still, small voice that we can hear if our ears and spirit are open to it. No matter how chaotic our lives become, God can hover over us and in His power calm the confusion, bringing peace into our lives.

What we must remember each moment is that God is constantly with us. He is behind us, beside us, and within us before, during, and after all storms. Remember the storm Jesus' disciples got caught up in? In that situation, as the disciples panicked and asked their friend and teacher for help, He was able to speak to the storm, telling "the waves to calm down, and they did. The sea became still and calm once again" (Matthew 8:26 VOICE).

When you're caught up in a storm, when you begin to fear and panic, remember that God is mightier than any tornado that is twisting up your mind, soul, spirit, and body; that all you need to do to get through the storm is call out for God. And before you know it, you'll be sailing on calm seas.

Help me, Lord, to always remember that I need not fear the storms that crop up in my life. For You are more powerful than anything that comes against me, and can give me the calm and courage to ride it out.

37

Day 16
God of Greatness

Read Psalm 48

The Eternal is great and mighty, worthy of great praise
in the city of our True God, upon His holy mountain.
Situated high above, Mount Zion is beautiful to see. . . .
the city of the great King. . . . God, our True God,
forever and ever. . .will be our guide till the end.

PSALM 48:1–2, 14 VOICE

- When was the last time you praised God not for what He's done for you but because of His extreme and supreme greatness?

- What person, place, or thing in your life have you been putting on a higher pedestal than God? When you put that person, place, or thing next to God, how does it compare to His greatness?

- What thoughts fill your mind as you consider that your great big God will be with you, guiding you, forever and ever?

It seems as if people in the Bible need to be reminded repeatedly that their God is great and mighty, better and bigger than anything they could ever encounter, imagine, and create. We seem to need that same reminder. For far too often, we put other things and people on a higher pedestal than God.

Sometimes we pay more honor and attention to money than to God. We find ourselves working so hard that we forget to worship Him. Or we find ourselves investing more of our time in material things, families, or the latest love we've found. The next thing you know, those people and things have disappointed us and our world crumbles. We look up and the people, possessions, and positions we'd been investing our time and money in begin to wobble, fall, and shatter before our eyes. And we find ourselves running to God for help, comfort, guidance, support, provision, and love, remembering *He* is the one who is always there, who never changes, who will never leave or desert us, who has been with us since the beginning and will be there in the end.

Lord, thank You for being in my life, for being my friend and guide forever and ever.

Day 17
God the Protector

Read Psalm 91

He who dwells in the secret place of the Most High shall remain stable and fixed under the shadow of the Almighty [Whose power no foe can withstand]. I will say of the Lord, He is my Refuge and my Fortress, my God; on Him I lean and rely, and in Him I [confidently] trust!

<small>PSALM 91:1–2 AMPC</small>

- Going with the premise that the promises of Psalm 91 depend on your meeting the conditions of its first two verses, how often do you dwell in that secret place, abiding in God, acknowledging Him as your protector, and trusting Him for all?

- What is God rescuing you from today? How does it feel knowing that no matter what comes against you, you are safe in His arms?

- Which of the promises in this psalm are speaking most to your heart today? Why might that be?

There are so many promises, assurances, and comforts available to you in the Most High God, the one who helps you, lifts you, walks with you.

Today's psalm reminds you that as long as you dwell in God's shadow, making Him your refuge and fortress, the sole thing on which you can rely, you will be assured of rescue if you get caught in a trap. You will find protection under His great wings. God's faithfulness to you will be like "a shield around you, a rock-solid wall to protect you" (Psalm 91:4 VOICE). With God in your life, you need not be afraid of night terrors, plagues, darkness, and disasters. By making God your eternal refuge and home, no evil will come knocking at your door. In fact, angels following His commands will keep you safe. They'll hold you in their hands so that you won't crash and burn when you trip over a stone.

God promises that if you cling to Him, He will rescue you, setting you above danger. When you call upon Him, He will answer, stay with you through the roughest patches. God, the one who gives His all to you, is all you need to live this life and enter the next one.

Lord, I come to You today, wanting to dwell in You, my refuge and fortress, the one on whom I lean and rely forever and ever. Amen.

Day 18
God of Refuge

Read Psalm 94

*I cried out, "I am slipping!" but your unfailing love,
O LORD, supported me. When doubts filled my mind, your
comfort gave me renewed hope and cheer. . . . The LORD
is my fortress; my God is the mighty rock where I hide.*
PSALM 94:18–19, 22 NLT

- In what ways do God's words, ways, and promises provide a refuge of relief for you in troubled times?

- When have you cried out to God that you were slipping, and His love supported you? When doubts filled your mind, in what ways did God comfort you and give you hope?

- How does it make you feel to know that in times of trouble, you have a place to go? What do you do to get to that place?

Here you are, doing what God would have you do, living your life for Him, trying to do the right thing. But then you take a look around and see how those doing wrong, the wicked people, are experiencing victory after victory, while you continue to struggle to keep your head above water, your career moving forward, food on the table, kids in line, and your marriage successful.

It's almost as if the wicked think that God doesn't see what they're doing, doesn't notice that they are harming defenseless widows and orphans. But then you think again. You remember that the God who formed the ear hears what they're doing and the cries of those they are hurting. The God who formed the eye sees what's happening. The God who created all creatures knows their thoughts and plans.

Know that God will bring justice to the wicked someday, that they will pay for their wrongs. Meanwhile, while they wreak havoc, you can stay safe in God, knowing He's supporting you with His love, renewing your hope and cheer, defending you from all that may harm you.

When things get tough, run to your piece of heaven on earth—God, your eternal refuge.

Thank You, Lord, for always being there for me, saving me with Your love, comforting me by renewing my hope and cheer, defending me from harm.

Day 19
God of Deliverance

Read Psalm 118

The Lord is my Strength and Song; and He has become my Salvation. . . . I will confess, praise, and give thanks to You, for You have heard and answered me; and You have become my Salvation and Deliverer.

PSALM 118:14, 21 AMPC

- God's mercy, faithful love, and kindness are forever. How does it feel knowing those things will follow you wherever you go?

- When was the last time you called on God while you were in dire straits? How did His answer, His deliverance of you, help you find better footing?

- What would happen if you began each morning knowing God is greater than anything you may face, rejoicing in the day He has made, and setting your intention to be glad in it?

Knowing God will deliver you from whatever has assailed or is assailing you is a continual confidence and courage booster. Knowing He is bigger and mightier than whatever problem or obstacle is standing in your way is a major faith builder.

You can boldly say, "GOD's now at my side and I'm not afraid; who would dare lay a hand on me? GOD's my strong champion; I flick off my enemies like flies" (Psalm 118:6–7 MSG).

Faithful female follower, always remember that it is so much "better to take refuge in GOD than trust in people; far better to take refuge in GOD than trust in celebrities" (Psalm 118:8–9 MSG). For people cannot do what your God can. Human heroes and celebrities may seem high and mighty but are short and shallow when compared to your Deliverer. It is God's hand, His power, His strength that will turn the tide in any battle you face. And it is God who will pick up the line when you call, wanting to hear your voice and save you from whatever has come against you.

Today, remember who your true Deliverer is. Then trust in Him to constantly and continually save you—from harm, from others, from yourself.

Lord, I turn myself and my life over to You. For You are the only one who can deliver me, the only one I can truly trust, the only one who will pick up the line every time I call!

Day 20
God of Purpose

Read Isaiah 42:1–9

I the Lord have called You [the Messiah] for a righteous purpose and in righteousness; I will take You by the hand and will keep You; I will give You for a covenant to the people [Israel], for a light to the nations [Gentiles], to open the eyes of the blind, to bring out prisoners from the dungeon, and those who sit in darkness from the prison.

ISAIAH 42:6–7 AMPC

- God supported Jesus Christ, put His Spirit upon Him, and held His hand as He opened the eyes of the blind and freed prisoners. What thoughts and feelings arise with that knowledge?

- It is God who gives you breath as you stand upon the earth and spirit as you walk upon it. When do you feel this the most?

- What new things is God doing in your life?

God has a purpose for all His creation. To help those made in His image get close to Him once more, He sent Jesus to earth to be a part of His covenant to the people of Israel, a light to the Gentiles. He sent Jesus to open the eyes of the blind and bring prisoners out of the darkness.

Just as God had a purpose for Jesus, He has a purpose for you. He put you here in this time and place for a reason. You have the opportunity to ask God what He would have you do, where He would have you go, what He would have you say. In so doing, you may understand, little by little, what role He wants you to play.

Today, seek God out. Request that He give you the guidance you need so that you can determine if He wants you to stay on your present road or take a detour. Knock on His door to understand what opportunities He wants you to take advantage of. Consider offering your big ASK (ask, seek, and knock) in the evening, just before bed. Then on the following morning, keep your eyes, ears, and heart open to His direction. Do so on purpose with His purpose for you in mind and spirit.

Here I am, Lord, coming before You. Reveal Your purpose for me in this time and place. Set my eyes on what I seek, my feet upon Your pathway, my hand upon Your door.

Day 21
God of Forgiveness

Read Isaiah 43:22–44:5

So let's get this clear: it's for My own sake that I save you. I am He who wipes the slate clean and erases your wrongdoing. I will not call to mind your sins anymore.

Isaiah 43:25 voice

- What thoughts arise as you consider that God forgives your sins, forgets your mistakes, not because of your character but because of His own? That, in spite of your sins, God continues to bless you in every way?

- What things might you need to confess to God today, things that you may not have even confessed to yourself?

- In what ways can you praise God for His amazingly generous gift of forgiving and forgetting?

God's forgiveness is free. That's why He wipes clear your sins, erases your errors. He is moved to do so not because of your merit but because of His mercy. That's how much your Creator loves you and wants the best for you.

Consider this: Is there anyone else in your life who is as selfless as your God? Is there anyone else in your life who loves you without exception?

Your God is ready, willing, and able to forgive you and wipe your record clean. To remember your misdeeds, wrong thoughts, and harmful words no more, to not even bring them up ever again. Yet when you do mess up in thought, word, or deed, you may still have to pay the consequences. Though when you find yourself in a flood or in the midst of a fire because you made a mistake (the consequences), He will still be there to rescue you from the water and the flames. Why? Because He cannot help but love you, His daughter, the apple of His eye.

Of course, you can never pay God back for all He has done for you. But you can give Him all the praise for being so loving and forgiving, above and beyond what you could ever hope or imagine.

---

*Lord, I have something I need to get off
my chest. Please forgive me for. . .*

Day 22
God the Servant

Read John 13:1–17

*I tell you the truth: a servant is not greater than the
master. Those who are sent are not greater than the
one who sends them. If you know these things, and if
you put them into practice, you will find happiness.*

JOHN 13:16–17 VOICE

- God, the master of the universe, as Jesus, donned an apron
  and got down on His knees to dig out the dirt between
  the toes and dry the scaly bottoms of the feet of people no
  better or worse than you. When was the last time you did
  something as servile or as humbling? How did that feel?

- In what ways do you humbly yet happily serve others?
  What blessings have you experienced in doing so?

Imagine knowing that you are shortly to die. Soon you will
voluntarily be leaving your friends and family. And before you
go, you know who it is who will betray you to your enemy,
leading to your agonizing death. Yet you also know there is
one big impression you can make upon the minds and hearts
of your followers, one last lesson you can teach them as they
continue on without you.

So you don an apron. You pour some water into a basin. And you begin gently and thoroughly to wash and dry your friends' feet, a task only the lowliest of servants would perform.

This is what your Lord and Master Jesus did before He began the long walk to His death. This is the lesson He wants you to learn. Jesus wants all His followers to be as humble and loving as He is, for these qualities are of the utmost importance to those who claim to be Christians. He wants those He has blessed to be a blessing to others, to serve as He served, and to lead as He led.

How would your day, your week, your month, your year, your life change if you walked this earth showing love and humility to everyone you encountered? How would their lives change?

I want to walk as You walked, Jesus. Help me find my happiness by loving and humbly serving others as You did.

51

Day 23
God of the Trinity

Read John 14

*The Father is sending a great Helper, the Holy Spirit,
in My name to teach you everything and to remind
you of all I have said to you. My peace is the legacy I
leave to you. I don't give gifts like those of this world.
Do not let your heart be troubled or fearful.*

JOHN 14:26–27 VOICE

- Jesus said that if you have seen Him, you have seen the Father. How does that change your present perception of God Himself?

- Consider Jesus' saying that if you believe in Him, you will do even greater things than He did and that whatever you ask, praying in His name, you'll receive. In what ways does knowing this give you the peace Jesus promises?

- The Holy Spirit has many names, such as Comforter, Helper, and Spirit of Truth. By which name do you know Him best? Why?

Imagine going through life untroubled and unafraid. That's what Jesus promises you. He makes it clear that He is the Son of the Father. And that although He, Jesus, must soon leave, His Father will send you someone to help you along the way. That someone is the Holy Spirit, the one who will help you through every stage of your life.

You, a daughter of God, the High King, are never alone in this life. There are three members of the Trinity who are beside you, within you, around you. They bring with them angels who will make sure you remain unharmed. This three-in-one God provides you with the Word so that you will find solace, comfort, guidance, and help in your time of need.

Too quickly we let the events of this world overtake us, make us feel as if we are helpless. The decisions we must make, at times, leave us uncertain as to which path to take. The relationships in our lives also often present challenges. That's why we need the Father, Son, and Spirit to aid us in our walk. We must have faith that they are always with us. They long for us to trust in them, knowing that when we do, we'll have the peace and courage we long for.

Three-in-one God, thank You for allowing me to tap into Your power, Spirit, and Word. Lead me to a life where I have the courage and calm to walk according to Your will.

Day 24
God the Life Giver

Read John 15:1–16:16

If you live in Me [abide vitally united to Me] and My words remain in you and continue to live in your hearts, ask whatever you will, and it shall be done for you.

<small>JOHN 15:7 AMPC</small>

- Jesus says that to bear fruit, you must abide or dwell in Him. For without Him, you can do nothing. How has this been tested and proven in your own life?

- What thoughts come up when you consider you did not choose Jesus but He chose you to bear fruit and receive whatever you ask for in prayer?

- Reflect on the fact that Jesus loves you and has sent the Holy Spirit to help guide you. In what ways does this give you life?

Jesus has sent not only the Holy Spirit to help you but provides you with the power of His Word. In John 15:7, Jesus makes clear that not only are you to stay connected to Him but to plant His words in your heart and live them out.

When you're connected to Jesus, you place yourself in a position of being loved and allowing that love to spill out of you and on to others. You are also linked up with the Holy Spirit, who will guide you in every aspect of life.

Even more important is planting Jesus' words in your heart. For His words will give you the right attitude and altitude. You will find kindness, love, and humility becoming your own attributes. And you will begin seeing your life and this world from a heavenly perspective.

So how do you plant Jesus' words in your heart? You read from the Bible each and every day. You find a verse that has a particular potency for you, and you memorize it so that it remains written on your heart and mind. As you do this verse by verse, day by day, you will be building a reservoir of wisdom, love, guidance, and peace within your heart. So that the next time you come up against a challenging situation or need to know which way to turn, you already have the answer and solution you seek within.

---

*Lord, open my eyes, heart, mind, and spirit to
the word You would have me know. Help me to
understand it, savor it, and plant it within so that
I can lead the life You would have me lead.*

Day 25
God the Savior

Read John 19:1–37

*When Jesus saw his mother standing there beside the
disciple he loved, he said to her, "Dear woman, here is your
son." And he said to this disciple, "Here is your mother."
And from then on this disciple took her into his home.*

JOHN 19:26–27 NLT

- How might this story have turned out differently if the
  people who played a role in ultimately executing Jesus had
  really known Him—as God the Savior?

- Why might it be difficult, emotionally and spiritually, to
  read this account? What could make reading it easier?

- Who in this story do you find hardest to identify with? The
  easiest to identify with? Besides Jesus, of whom are you
  the proudest? Of whom are you the most ashamed? What
  qualities might you share with each of these characters?

Jesus did not lose His life. He gave it up voluntarily. Why?
So that you could live and love as He did. So that you would
have access to the Helper (a.k.a. Holy Spirit). So that you
could have a connection with God that can never be broken.

Yet still, the account of Jesus' crucifixion can be difficult to read. We cannot help but feel for the Man who was so abused in His last days. Yet we cannot lose ourselves in the sorrow of the moment. Instead, we must take in the lessons that Jesus is trying to teach those who come after Him.

One of those lessons is to love no matter what we are going through. To see others through the eyes of humility and care. For it was in Jesus' last moments that He looked out at the crowd around Him and saw His mother's face, as well as that of the disciple He loved (presumably John). He did not allow His pain and agony to twist the love He carried. Instead, He made sure that His beloved mother would be taken care of by putting her in the hands of the disciple He cherished and who stuck with Him to the end.

Every day, may you take this lesson of love to heart and use it to love those around you.

Jesus, thank You for saving me. Thank You
for loving me beyond comprehension. Help
me to do the same in my own life.

Day 26
God of the Resurrection

Read Mark 16

Do not be amazed and terrified; you are looking for Jesus of Nazareth, Who was crucified. He has risen; He is not here. See the place where they laid Him. But be going; tell the disciples and Peter, He goes before you into Galilee; you will see Him there, [just] as He told you.

<small>MARK 16:6–7 AMPC</small>

- The female followers of Jesus were the first to arrive at His tomb, ready to go about the normal duties following the death of a loved one. They were shocked to find the door of the tomb rolled away. When were you last going about your normal duties and surprised by the God of the resurrection? Did you run away in fright and disbelief, or did you stay to hear His message?

- When did you first believe in the resurrected God? How is He working with you today?

Jesus had been crucified and placed in a tomb. Over that tomb was a rock, which the women were certain they would not be able to roll away. But when they arrived on the scene, the stone was already rolled back. What they had been afraid of, what they had feared, was no longer an issue.

How often do you waste your time worrying about things you don't need to worry about? Questions are rattling around in your mind that need not be answered because the assumed "problem" never materializes.

This account of the women arriving at the tomb teaches us another lesson: Not only are many fears groundless, but the things Jesus has told His followers are truth. He told His disciples He would rise again. Yet there was apparently some doubt in their minds as to the reality of His words.

Interestingly enough, the *women* who visited the empty tomb did not doubt Jesus' words, nor those of the angel they encountered there. Mary Magdalene, the first person to whom Jesus appeared, "brought this news back to all those who had followed Him and were still mourning and weeping, but they refused to believe she had seen Jesus alive" (Mark 16:10–11 VOICE) until Jesus appeared to them personally.

You are a woman of sense and purpose. You are a follower of Jesus. Believe His words, take them as facts, and use them to steer and define your life.

Risen Christ, in You and Your words I believe.
May they continually steer my life and heart.

Day 27
God Our Friend

Read 1 John 1:1–2:14

This is the message we heard from Jesus and now declare to you: God is light, and there is no darkness in him at all. . . . If we are living in the light, as God is in the light, then we have fellowship with each other, and the blood of Jesus, his Son, cleanses us from all sin.

1 JOHN 1:5, 7 NLT

- Imagine God your friend loving you so much that He came down to earth to show you the way back to Him. You can now be a friend to Him like Eve and her fellow creation Adam were before the Fall. How does knowing God loves you so much help you to love and befriend your fellow people?

- In what ways can you keep your connection to the light of God shining through you and onto others during the darkest of times?

How wonderful to have a friend in Jesus. To know someone who loves you so much that He allowed His life to be sacrificed so that you could have a one-on-one relationship with God.

Let's face it. We're not perfect. But Jesus is. And it is He who gave us the ability to unburden our hearts, to tell Him of all the wrongs we have done, and not just forgive us for them but actually wipe our record clean—and continue to love us more than we perhaps deserve. That is the friend we have in Jesus. That is the love He has shown by giving up His life for us, the love He continually shows by extending us forgiveness.

On those days when you feel like you can't do anything right, during those times when you don't even love yourself very much, stop thinking, doing, and blaming. Instead, turn to Jesus. Confess your shortcomings and mistakes. Ask Him to shower upon you His eternal love and forgiveness. Then take that same love and forgiveness He has poured down upon you, absorb what you need, and use the rest to pour into someone else's life. Be that friend in Jesus that He is to you.

Pardon me, my Lord and friend, for all the ways I have erred. Pour Your love and forgiveness down upon me and help me use the excess to befriend another in You.

Day 28
God the Praiseworthy

Read Revelation 4:1–5:14

When he took the scroll, the four living beings and the twenty-four elders fell down before the Lamb. Each one had a harp, and they held gold bowls filled with incense, which are the prayers of God's people. And they sang a new song.

REVELATION 5:8–9 NLT

- In what ways do you express your praise when you look through the heavenly door standing open in your own mind and see God sitting on His throne?

- What three features or aspects of God bring out the most praise in you?

- Envision your prayers being in the golden bowls of incense held by heavenly creatures who are singing songs of praise to Jesus the Lamb. How does that make you feel? What song might you write today to express your praise to God?

In this moment, consider what words you'd like to say, what you want to offer God. Get them formulated in your mind. Then, as you say those words, as you lift them up to the Lord, imagine your prayers appearing to God in the form of incense as it wafts up to His waiting ears.

Jesus has given you the ability to raise your prayers up to the heavens and allow them to land in God's ears. What a privilege! What a miracle! What a system! What a blessing!

You have been given the chance to speak to God each moment of every day. Jesus sacrificed His life for this connection between you and the holiest of holies. He would not have you neglect this privilege.

In recognition of that divine honor of praying to the Most High, some praises are in order. And how wonderful to take advantage of that holy opportunity by joining in with all the other heavenly beings as they praise the one who created, maintains, and sustains the universe and everything in it—including you. What will you offer to Him today?

To the one who sits on the throne and the Lamb beside Him, may I sing a new song filled with blessing, honor, glory, and power in this moment and throughout the ages!

Day 29
God of Salvation

Read Revelation 19

And again their voices rang out: "Praise the LORD! The smoke from that city ascends forever and ever!" Then the twenty-four elders and the four living beings fell down and worshiped God, who was sitting on the throne. They cried out, "Amen! Praise the LORD!" And from the throne came a voice that said, "Praise our God, all his servants."

REVELATION 19:3–5 NLT

- Within the first four verses of this reading, three times various heavenly creatures shout "Alleluia!" for the God of salvation, praising His victory. Consider doing so yourself, right now joining in with them, then recording your thoughts and feelings—before and after your shouts of your own "Alleluia!"

- Imagine heaven opening, revealing a white horse with a rider called Faithful and True. It's Jesus, the Son of God, who defeats all evil—saving your very life, spirit and soul. What words of praise do you have for Him?

Praise. When is the last time you praised God for something? Not thanked Him for doing anything for you but just to praise

Him? From the very core of your being? If it takes you awhile to answer this question, you might want to consider making praise to God a part of your day every day.

There are several reasons praise is good for you *and* God. One is that the Bible says you should (Psalm 34:1; 150:1-6; James 5:13), continually. Another reason is that praising God takes you out of yourself and brings you before His throne—and not just to have another request granted but simply because you want to let Him know how great you think He is. Another reason to praise God is because He is worthy to be praised (Psalm 145). Another is because praise from your lips and heart helps the earth to increase her productivity so that she yields a bountiful harvest (Psalm 67:4–7).

Today and every day, sit yourself down, dig deep into your heart, and then look up at the heavens. Find some words of praise to take you out of yourself and into God. As you do, your perspective, productivity, and passion for God will move mountains within and without.

I come before You today, Lord, with praise
on my lips, offered from my heart.

65

Day 30
God the Approachable

Read Revelation 22

And the throne of God and of the Lamb will sit prominently in the city. God's servants will continually serve and worship Him. They will be able to look upon His face, and His name will be written on their foreheads. Darkness will never again fall on this city.

REVELATION 22:3–5 VOICE

- Someday you will find yourself eternally dwelling with God in a beautiful place, having a relationship with Him like Eve had before the Fall. What might be one of the first things you say or do when you see God face-to-face?

- In what ways do you acknowledge God's presence in your everyday doings? How do you approach Him?

- Now that you have gotten to know God better, how much more is He revealing in your life? What's the most important thing He wants you to know?

It may be a while before you get to see God and Jesus sitting on the throne in the New City of Jerusalem, but it's nice to think about it while you're walking God's way through this world.

So why not do some brainstorming today? Consider living with God in eternity, in one of the most beautiful places you've ever seen. What would you like to ask God? What would you like to tell Him?

In the meantime, while you're still earthbound, why not approach God in the present? Why not envision Him on His throne, busy with all the earth and her peoples' doings yet still ready to bend an ear whenever you call His name, ready to lend a helping hand, putting up shields of protection around you to keep you safe from unseen forces?

Consider all that God does without you even asking. Think about all the ways He provides for you—spiritually and physically. In fact, keep Him on your mind every second of the day, knowing His love and forgiveness, His kindness and protection are there for you 24/7 and beyond.

Thank You, God, for standing so close to me, for keeping Your hand upon me, for watching out for me. Let's spend every moment of this day together.

30 Days of Bible Readings for Knowing Jesus Better

I want to know Christ and experience the mighty power that raised him from the dead.
PHILIPPIANS 3:10 NLT

Jesus. To know Him is to love Him—and realize His love for you. From His humble earthly beginning to His spectacular supernatural never-ending, He is calling you to a purpose you can only begin to imagine.

In this second of three 30-day Bible reading plans, from Jesus' birth in the manger to His vacating the tomb, you will be exploring scriptures to better understand the Jewish leader, preacher, and teacher who forever transformed—and continues to transform—the world and the people in it.

As you approach your Bible reading each day, allow God's Word to speak for itself. Start off with a simple prayer, something like "Here I am, Lord, ready to listen and learn, to hear and heed You. Let Your light shine upon me, my heart, mind, spirit, and soul." Then read that day's passage, intending to hear Jesus' voice. Meditate upon the Word. Underline the verse or passage that stands out to you the most. Then, and only then, expecting Christ to reveal Himself, read and reflect upon the questions from that day's reading. Afterward, read that day's devotion and pray, thanking God for this time together, asking Him to help you apply what you've learned to your life and heart and to follow where He's leading.

Day 1
The Birth of Jesus (Part 1)

Read Matthew 1:18–25

Joseph. . .decided to break the engagement quietly. As he considered this, an angel of the Lord appeared to him in a dream. "Joseph, son of David," the angel said, "do not be afraid to take Mary as your wife. For the child within her was conceived by the Holy Spirit."

MATTHEW 1:19–20 NLT

- When has God stepped into your dreams and rerouted you amid one of your best-laid plans? Did you heed God's redirection or stick staunchly to your already well laid-out path?

- Have you obeyed God in a situation where He asks you to do what seems to go against tradition, public opinion, and societal norms? What was the result?

- How do your expectations and God's plans differ? How do you allow room for God to speak into your life, separating your inner chatter from His divine voice?

God can speak into our lives in many ways—through His Word, His promises, His people, and His angels, just to name a few. And if we are open to these sources and apply ourselves to act on God's messages, we find ourselves on God's pathway for us, the one He has planned from the beginning.

In today's scripture, Joseph had made a decision based on mortal facts in the mortal world. Chances are he went to sleep that evening with this situation weighing heavily on his mind. Yet he was obviously a man of God, for that night when the angel spoke to Joseph in a dream, he took the angel's words to heart. This heavenly messenger more fully explained to him the situation in which the mortal found himself. He was, in effect, given the backstory of Mary's pregnancy and learned it was gained through God's power. When Joseph woke the next day, he had a new plan of action and took Mary to be his wife.

Know that God speaks to you in a myriad of ways. Understand that although you may have made a certain decision, you need to be flexible when God, in His own unique way and timing, gives you a different direction or game plan. In all matters of the spirit, heart, mind, and soul, going God's way is always the best way.

Lord, help me stay open to hearing, acknowledging, and following Your guidance, in whatever form it takes.

Day 2

The Birth of Jesus (Part 2)

Read Luke 2:1–20

After they saw the baby, they spread the story of what they had experienced and what had been said to them about this child. Everyone who heard their story couldn't stop thinking about its meaning. Mary, too, pondered all of these events, treasuring each memory in her heart.

LUKE 2:16–19 VOICE

- When have you discovered God's glory and richness during an ordinary life event set amid seemingly dire circumstances? What joy did that bring you?

- Which unexpected happenings, things that startled you, prompted you to ponder God's amazing orchestration of life events?

- How does it change your perspective knowing that God often uses the most ordinary and lowliest of messengers to bring great goodwill and good news into the world, touching the hearts and changing the lives of others forevermore?

Shepherds had been in fields outside of Bethlehem, taking care of their flocks in the night, guarding them from predators. Then suddenly a messenger of the Lord stood before them and gave the shepherds—society's lowliest of the low—a message: "Don't be afraid! Listen! I bring good news of great joy" (Luke 2:10 VOICE). The messenger told them that in the City of David a child was born, the Son of God, who would free them from their sins. The messenger gave them the details of where and when they would know the child.

That first messenger was then surrounded by thousands of others, who praised God, giving Him all the glory. And then they were gone.

Reeling from what they'd witnessed, the stupefied and intrigued shepherds went to check out the message and found things were just as they'd been told. For they'd found, seen, and met Mary, Joseph, and the baby. That's when the shepherds began spreading their amazing story—and all who heard it couldn't stop thinking about it.

In the beginning of His Son's earthly life, God sent a message about the newly born Savior to lowly shepherds. When Jesus was resurrected, the message of His resurrection was given to a common woman, Mary Magdalene. What message from God will you convey to others—and then give all the glory for its results back to Him?

---

*Thank You, Lord, for using the humble like me
to spread the joy of Your message to others.*

Day 3
Visit of the Wise Men

Read Matthew 2:1–12

Not long after Jesus was born, magi, wise men or seers from the East, made their way from the East to Jerusalem. These wise men made inquiries.
Wise Men: *Where is this newborn, who is the King of the Jews? When we were far away in the East we saw His star, and we have followed its glisten and gleam all this way to worship Him.*

<small>MATTHEW 2:1–2 VOICE</small>

- In what ways do you feel you've had to travel far to find and worship Jesus, the King? What did your searching reveal?

- When was the last time you took a gift to Jesus? What was its significance to you? How do you think it was received?

- When was the last time God warned you about something while you were dreaming or when you were in a physically, spiritually, and mentally receptive state? Were you able to allow God's counsel to override your womanly wisdom and intuition?

After Jesus' birth, the glistening and gleaming star that hung over Him attracted the attention of three wise men. So they followed its light and, like any normal travelers, began to question others as to where the newborn King of the Jews might be found so that they could worship Him.

This news about another king worried the earthly ruler Herod. So he sent the wise men to Bethlehem, telling them to search for the babe there and then let him know so he could worship Him. Yet what he really wanted was the location of the newborn so he could have Him killed.

The wise men did find the baby Jesus. They did worship Him and give Him gifts. Then God warned the men in a dream to not go back to Herod but to travel home another way.

When you're following the light of Jesus, you too may be misled by fellow earthlings. So stay open to God's wisdom, His messages, His advice so that you'll be able to easily change course when needed.

Thank You, Lord, for sending Your light to lead me where You would have me go. May I always be open and looking for Your guidance and wisdom as I take this journey of life with You within and without.

Day 4
The Word Became Flesh

Read John 1:1–28

The Word was first, the Word present to God, God present to the Word. . . . Everything was created through him; nothing—not one thing!—came into being without him. What came into existence was Life, and the Life was Light to live by. The Life-Light blazed out of the darkness; the darkness couldn't put it out.

JOHN 1:1–5 MSG

- What does it mean to you that Jesus is *the* Word who speaks all things into being and sustains all things—including you? What is Jesus speaking and sustaining in your life today?

- What words or feelings come to mind when you realize that *because you believe in Jesus, you are God's daughter* and have all the birthrights and privileges that connection entails?

- When have you felt like John the Baptist, a lone voice crying in the wilderness?

There is no darkness that can put out the "Life-Light" that is Jesus. And because He is also the Word—the one who spoke all things into being and continues to sustain and maintain them forever—nothing will be able to ever drown out or erase that Word.

How wonderful to have something in this life that's stable, that's forever, that's unchanging, unmoving, unalterable; to believe in a God of light who can never be overshadowed by anything else in heaven or on earth.

Whenever you feel lost or alone, remember there's a Light before you, within you, around you, one that can be prayed to, praised, one that will listen and raise. When your thoughts threaten to take you down, lift them up to the Life-Light and ask Him, who is also the Word, to replace your thoughts with His thoughts, to renew your mind, heart, spirit, soul, and self-speak.

Know that because you are God's daughter, you have constant access to all the Light you need and all the Word you crave. Ask Him to speak into your life what you need to hear, know, and understand today.

Shine Your light, Lord, into my heart. Illuminate any darkness You find within, transforming me into a being like You. Touch my thoughts and replace them with Your Word. In Jesus' name, amen.

Day 5
A Light Has Risen

Read Matthew 4:12–17

*In the land of Zebulun and the land of Naphtali, the
road to the sea along the Jordan in Galilee, the land of the
outsiders—in these places, the people who had been living
in darkness saw a great light. The light of life will overtake
those who dwelt in the shadowy darkness of death.*

MATTHEW 4:15–16 VOICE

- When have you felt as if you were being swallowed up
  by darkness? What were you thinking and feeling at the
  time? How did you get back into the light?

- Where do you go when you are discouraged, when those
  you love are imprisoned spiritually, emotionally, mentally,
  or physically? How or why does that place soothe you?

- What are some of the Bible verses you rely on to keep
  you from being overcome by the darkness? How does the
  Word keep you in the light?

Ever feel like an outsider? That's how the Gentiles must have
felt—kingless, lightless, hopeless. And then came this man
who was considered the king of all people, the light of all the
world, the hope of the hopeless. This king who would reign

over the hearts of all those walking upon the earth.

Perhaps before you came to Christ you felt a little lost and alone, a little bit "in the dark." And then you walked into a church or stumbled upon a Bible. Or perhaps you met someone in whom you saw something you wanted, an undefinable otherworldliness that you wanted to tap into. Whatever your entrance into a community of faith, you saw the light for which deep down you had always longed. For the first time you felt like an insider instead of an outsider, someone more at home with God than anyone or anywhere else.

Today, remember whose you are. Remember where you belong. Seek out that risen light once more and allow it to revive your sense of community, the lightness of being, and the hope that refreshes and renews.

---

*Lord, pull me close to Your light. Warm my heart
with Your Word. Keep me close, in this community
of believers, the one blessed with hope in You.*

Day 6
Jesus' Ministry in Galilee

Read Luke 4:14–37

*God's Spirit is on me; he's chosen me to preach
the Message of good news to the poor, sent me to
announce pardon to prisoners and recovery of sight
to the blind, to set the burdened and battered free,
to announce, "This is God's time to shine!"*

LUKE 4:18–19 MSG

- Is it your custom, as it was Jesus' (see Luke 4:16), to go to church every week? Why or why not?

- When, if ever, have you gone "home" and been treated with disdain by the people there because of your faith? Were you able to pass through their midst and go on your way? What gave you the power to do so?

- In what situations has Jesus come and healed your broken heart? Liberated your imprisoned spirit? Given your mind new insight? Set your soul free from oppression?

No matter how you feel or are faring, Jesus is here to help. How do we know that? Because He said so.

When Jesus went back to His hometown, He went to the local synagogue, as He was always wont to do on the

Sabbath, and there He stood up and read from the book of Isaiah. He told the people that the passage selected, the one He had read aloud, was just fulfilled. That He was the one who the Spirit of God was upon. That He had been chosen to preach the good news to the poor, to pardon the prisoners and restore sight to the blind, to free those burdened and battered, to let people know that God's favor had arrived.

That is who Jesus can be to you if you let Him. God's Son, His representative in the flesh, has a message for you when you need direction. He can free you from any prison within and without. He can restore your sight and free you of whatever is burdening you. He is the conduit to God's grace.

Today, know that Jesus is here, at home in you, waiting to help you, heal you, move you. Will you let Him?

Here I am, Jesus, drawn to the light and Spirit of God You emit. Help me, heal me, love me.

Day 7
Jesus' True Family

Read Mark 3:13–35

He climbed a mountain and invited those he wanted with him. . . . Looking around, taking in everyone seated around him, he said, "Right here, right in front of you—my mother and my brothers. Obedience is thicker than blood. The person who obeys God's will is my brother and sister and mother."

MARK 3:13, 33–35 MSG

- Jesus calls to Himself those He wants to work with Him. When did Jesus call you? How has your life changed as a result?

- To what has Jesus called you to work with Him? How do you tap into His power to fulfill that calling?

- Those who do God's will are Jesus' brother, sister, and mother. How does it feel to claim that privilege? How would your life perspective change if you keep your role as His sister or mother uppermost in your thoughts?

Jesus has invited those He wants to come with Him. You are one of that number. You have been called to follow Him. And if you do follow Him, if you obey Him, you will become part of His family, taking on the role of Jesus' sister or mother.

Imagine that! Because you are a part of Jesus' family, you will never ever be alone. You will never be without help, support, love, and friendship.

Yet as a member of that family of God, you do have a role to play. You are a part of God's good plan for all His children—of which you are one. And God has all you need to fulfill the part you have been brought to play here in this time and place.

Each day gives you the opportunity to serve God in a specific way with your specific talent. If you are unsure what your role or gift is, go to God. Ask Him to help you find your specific spiritual gift. Ask Him what He would have you do in this time and place. Know that direction will be provided. Your job is to open yourself to it and obediently follow wherever He leads.

I am honored, Lord, to be a part of Your family.
Help me use my gifts as I follow wherever You lead.

Day 8
Jesus Cleanses the Temple and Meets with Nicodemus

Read John 2:12–3:21

Many people noticed the signs he was displaying and, seeing they pointed straight to God, entrusted their lives to him. But Jesus didn't entrust his life to them. He knew them inside and out, knew how untrustworthy they were. He didn't need any help in seeing right through them.

JOHN 2:23–25 MSG

- In what ways have you given material things and mental "transactions" priority over prayer and worship within your own temple of God?

- What thoughts and feelings arise when you realize that Jesus knows exactly what is in your heart and mind?

- What changes occurred in your life after your spirit was born of God's Spirit? How do you nourish the "new you"?

During Passover, Jesus was in Jerusalem. While there, many people noticed the miracles He was performing. Because of those miracles, they began to believe in Him, trust in Him. But for many this was a one-time-only occasion. Their belief was a surface faith. And Jesus, knowing the human heart inside out, realized He couldn't trust these surface-faith believers with His life and plan, as He did the disciples.

It takes knowledge of the Word to understand who Christ is. And that understanding is gained by reading the Word, hearing it, and meditating upon it. After that knowledge of Christ is gained, a deeper faith is felt, and an individual can then fully entrust her life to Jesus, and Jesus, in turn, can then entrust Himself to her, taking her deeper and deeper into God's plan and her part in it.

Jesus knows your heart. He knows the doubts you entertain, the worries that plague you, the uncertainties that make you hesitate to trust Him fully. Today, ask Jesus to help you assuage your doubts. Ask Him to look deep into your heart and help you root out the uncertainties that keep bubbling to the surface. Then ask Him to take you deeper so that you can find the path He has trod before you, the one He wants you to embark on as you follow Him.

Lord, help me find a way to go deeper into my faith in You.

Day 9
Parables of Jesus

Read Mark 4:1–34

But those last seeds—those sown into good soil?
Those people hear the word, accept it, meditate on
it, act on it, and bear fruit—a crop 30, 60, or 100
times larger than the farmer dropped to earth.

<small>MARK 4:20 VOICE</small>

- Which of these parables is speaking most to your soul today? Why might that be?

- In what ways do you prepare the ground of your heart so that when the seed of God's Word falls on it, you are able to readily accept it and bear fruit because of it?

- How does it encourage you knowing that the more you think and study about what you read in God's Word, the more wisdom you will get out of it? How has that already been proven in your life?

In His parable about the farmer and the seeds, Jesus explains its meaning to His disciples by telling them that the seed the farmer is sowing is God's Word, the good news. The first group of people are the seed that's thrown onto the path and is snapped up by the evil one before it has a chance to take root. The second is seed thrown upon the rocks, representing the people who hear the Word with joy, but their faith withers up when troubles come.

The third group is represented by the seed that's tossed among weeds but is choked out, representing people whom God's Word has reached but it's choked out by "the things of this life—the worries, the drive for more and more, the desire for other things" (Mark 4:19 VOICE). The fourth group of people are represented by the seed sown upon good soil. They hear the Word and make it a part of their lives, enabling them to bear good fruit in abundance!

If you are in the fourth group and are bearing lots of fruit, praise God! If you are in one of the first three groups, it's time to take stock of your life, to find a way to get deeper into God's Word so that you can begin to bear a fruitful life. Start by asking Jesus for help and guidance.

Lord, I want to bear a more fruitful life for You.
Show me where to start, how to begin.

Day 10
The Heart of Humankind

Read Mark 7

He took the man off by himself, put his fingers in the man's ears and some spit on the man's tongue. Then Jesus looked up in prayer, groaned mightily, and commanded, "Ephphatha!—Open up!" And it happened. The man's hearing was clear and his speech plain—just like that.

MARK 7:33–35 MSG

- When might you have found yourself praising Jesus with your lips while your heart was far removed from Him? What feelings and thoughts come to mind when you consider that when your heart is aligned with Jesus' heart, there is no physical distance He cannot breach to answer your prayer?

- What are you persistently praying about in these days? How might God be using this experience in prayer to test your faith?

- What is Jesus commanding your heart to be opened to today?

Perhaps for some time you have been on your knees in prayer, asking God for a miracle, speaking to Him from your heart.

And yet nothing in your life seems to have changed. Your need, malady, conflict, problem, burden remains. Perhaps now it is time to follow Jesus' example of prayer.

When you have a heavy burden on your heart, get off by yourself, to a place where you can be totally alone, physically or spiritually. Then look up to the heavens. Imagine God looking down at you in love, bending His ear to listen with compassion. Allow whatever words or sounds are within you to rise up from the deepest part of your soul and spirit. Let God know your request, your pain, your anguish, your need, your heart. Draw down His power, knowing with all the faith you can muster that God does answer the prayers of His servants. Then wait for God's work to manifest itself into your physical world and spiritual heart. Know that "just like that" God can work a miracle in your life.

---

*Lord of my heart, I look up to You, knowing that
You see my situation, hear my pleas, know my pain,
can assuage my need. Allow me to draw down Your
power, knowing You will answer my prayer.*

Day 11
Equality with God

Read John 5

I tell you, the person whose ears are open to My words [who listens to My message] and believes and trusts in and clings to and relies on Him Who sent Me has (possesses now) eternal life. And he does not come into judgment [does not incur sentence of judgment, will not come under condemnation], but he has already passed over out of death into life.

JOHN 5:24 AMPC

- Although angels may stir healing waters to which you may walk, it is Jesus who, knowing you inside out, performs the whole healing. How might this change the spiritual order of things in your mind?

- Which more closely describes you: a follower of the rules or a follower of the Rule Maker? Which do you think is the better of the two?

- Because you have heard Jesus' Word and believe God sent Him, you have eternal life. What thoughts and feelings does this fact inspire?

Jesus describes the person who has already been given eternal life. She is one whose ears are open to Jesus' words, listens to

His message. Yet it goes deeper than that. The eternal-life liver must believe in God, the one who has sent Jesus with His message. She must trust in Him with all her heart, cling to Him with all her soul, and rely on Him deep in her spirit. It is that woman who is already living her eternal life in Jesus.

How many of those boxes can you tick? To be open to Jesus' words, you must immerse yourself in them. That in itself will help you in the other areas, boosting your belief, understanding more and more about Jesus and His mission. When problems come, you must cling tightly to God with all your soul, not letting doubts loosen your grip. You must rely on God from deep down within, not worrying over how He will provide or get you out of the jam you're in, remembering He knows what's happening and will save you in His time and His way, both of which may be beyond your imagining.

Today, meet with the Eternal, knowing He is watching, waiting to connect with His eternal daughter on this side of heaven and the next.

Lord, open my ears to Your Word, for it is in You I trust, to You I cling, on You I rely, forever and ever. Amen.

Day 12

Sermon on the Mount (Part 1)

Read Matthew 5

"In a word, what I'm saying is, Grow up. You're
kingdom subjects. Now live like it. Live out your
God-created identity. Live generously and graciously
toward others, the way God lives toward you."

MATTHEW 5:48 MSG

- Which of the "Blessed are" statements (see Matthew 5:3–10) apply to you today? How does that comfort or strengthen you?

- In what ways are you letting your light shine so that your good works can point others to God?

- Who is Jesus prompting you to forgive today? For whom are you to go the second mile? Which enemy is He prompting you to bless? How does it feel to follow through on Jesus' promptings? How might your following Jesus' nudges every day become a habit?

We like to see ourselves as fully grown mature women, living our lives in Christ. Yet in today's verse, Jesus is basically telling us to "grow up"! After all, we're not just God's daughters but also subjects of His kingdom. That means we are servants of God Himself, the one who is the very personification of love. We are to live the way He wants us to live and be the women He wants us to be.

Jesus reminds us that it's easy for us to love our friends. And then He challenges us to love even our enemies, allowing them to bring out the best, not the worst, of ourselves. When someone gives us a hard time, we're to pray for them, "for then you are working out of your true selves, your God-created selves. This is what God does. He gives his best. . .to everyone, regardless: the good and bad, the nice and nasty" (Matthew 5:44–45 MSG).

Although loving your enemies and doing good to those who treat you badly sounds like a major challenge, relax. God has you covered. He will give you the power and resources to do whatever He calls you to do.

---

*Help me every day, Lord, to be more and more
like You, loving the good and the bad, the nice
and the nasty. In Jesus' name. Amen.*

Day 13
Sermon on the Mount (Part 2)

Read Matthew 6

When you pray, go into a private room, close the door, and pray unseen to your Father who is unseen. Then your Father, who sees in secret, will reward you. And when you pray, do not go on and on. . . . Your prayers need not be labored or lengthy or grandiose—for your Father knows what you need before you ever ask Him.

MATTHEW 6:6–8 VOICE

- What behind-the-scenes, do-good deed can you perform for someone in your life, a deed that you keep just between you and God? After following through, what reward did you openly receive from God as a result?

- Where is your secret prayer closet? What is it like? How often do you use it?

- How does seeking first the kingdom of God help you forgive others, lay up treasures in heaven instead of earth, keep you loyal to God instead of money, and stave off worrying about tomorrow?

Jesus tells us to go into a private room and shut the door, to pray unseen by prying eyes, to speak to our Father who is also unseen and will reward us.

It may be that you have no place at home to call your own little corner or closet. That's okay. God knows what is happening in every aspect of your life. The important thing is that you pray secretly from within. In fact, if you have such a place within you, you can be in a room full of people, praying, and no one will know except you and Father God. You also don't have to worry about using a lot of words and motions in your requests to God. He doesn't need you to put on a show to get your point across.

We women usually have a lot going on in our lives, a lot of people to tend to, work for, raise, and rescue. So now that you know you can make anywhere you go your prayer closet, don't neglect it. Use it whenever you need to pray—for the kids, the husband, the parents, the in-laws, friends, and strangers, the loved and the seemingly unlovable—knowing that when you go deep within and pray heart to heart, God will hear and act.

Lord, hear my prayer. . .

Sermon on the Mount (Part 3)

Read Matthew 7

"Do not judge others, and you will not be judged. For you will be treated as you treat others. The standard you use in judging is the standard by which you will be judged."

MATTHEW 7:1–2 NLT

- What would your thoughts and words be like if you refrained from judging others? How might your doing so draw others closer to God?

- Only as you continually ask, seek, and knock will you receive, find, and have doors opened. How might keeping this in mind every day help you live a fuller life with God?

- How would your life change if you treated everyone—regardless of who they are or what they have done—just as *you* would want to be treated twenty-four hours a day?

Jesus reminds us in Matthew 7:1–2 that by whatever means we use to judge other people, we ourselves will be judged. This is a truth humans need to be reminded of often.

Imagine how little would actually come out of our mouths if we curbed our judging of others. And this is how Jesus would have us live, thus it is not in any way to be neglected.

Jesus truly brings this no-judging-allowed edict home when He asks us why we can manage to see the speck in someone else's eyes and be blind to the log we have in our own. He wonders how we can even think of offering to help another get rid of the speck in her eye when we can't see past the log in our own eye.

It's amazing how Jesus puts up with us and our shenanigans. How easy it is to criticize others when we have so many problems in our own lives.

Today, take Jesus' advice to heart. Find a way to remind yourself daily not to judge or criticize others. Instead, speak words of encouragement into their lives and keep your criticisms to yourself. And remember, Jesus will be only too willing to help you do as He asks.

Jesus, help me keep my words free of criticizing others, to treat others as I would want to be treated, to live as You would have me live and be whom You would have me be. Amen.

Day 15

Power over the Physical World

Read Luke 8:22–56

The disciples went and woke him up, shouting,
"Master, Master, we're going to drown!" When
Jesus woke up, he rebuked the wind and the raging
waves. Suddenly the storm stopped and all was calm.
Then he asked them, "Where is your faith?"

LUKE 8:24–25 NLT

- How does the fact that Jesus has the power to still the winds and waves calm you? How does the idea that Jesus is *always* in your boat help you face life's trials?

- When have you felt the power of Jesus stanching the flow of issues in your life? How has knowing that your faith has made you well bring you joy and peace?

- What power do the words "Don't be afraid, only believe" hold for you? How would life change if they were your mantra?

Today's world is full of tumult—wars, mass shootings, riots, assaults, hurricanes, global warming, pandemics. The list goes on and on. Every time you look at a newspaper, watch a news program, or catch up on world events on your favorite feed, your heart is liable to sink down to your feet. Tears may well up in your eyes. You may even begin to have a panic attack.

When you are caught up in the storms of life and have done all you can to rectify your situation, don't become frozen with fear. Instead, calmly apply to the Lord for help. Know that He is there with you, riding out the storm by your side. Know that He can bring calm into your heart and any situation you may find yourself in. He has the power and will stop the waves of terror and torment from sucking the joy out of your spirit. He may do so by giving you the words you need to hear, or He will simply stay silent, stand by your side, and slowly bring you back into a safe harbor.

Allow your trust in Jesus to take away any terrors this world may throw at you. Simply bring your faith to the fore, knowing that the one who can calm the wind and still the waves is able to bring you all the peace you need.

Lord, I'm coming to You for some help to
stay calm, cool, and collected in You.

Day 16
Power tò Heal (Part 1)

Read Matthew 8:1–17

But the officer said, "Lord, I am not worthy to have you come into my home. Just say the word from where you are, and my servant will be healed." . . . Then Jesus said to the Roman officer, "Go back home. Because you believed, it has happened." And the young servant was healed that same hour.

Matthew 8:8, 13 NLT

- When asking Jesus for healing, how are you like (or unlike) the leper who came to Him, worshipped Him, and then stated his faith by saying he knew Jesus could heal him if He was willing?

- Nothing impedes Jesus' healing power—neither time nor distance. What does that tell you about Jesus' role, presence, and power in your life?

- How does it feel knowing Jesus doesn't just heal you and those you love but actually takes all illnesses and injuries upon Himself?

Some days you may feel as if you are powerless. This is especially true when a loved one is ill and not near at hand. You cannot see her face, reach out and touch his hand, or press your lips against her forehead. These are the times when you need to reach deep down into your faith and seek to connect with Jesus.

In Matthew 8:5–13, we read about a Roman officer whose servant was ill. Jesus offered to follow him to his home, to go there and heal him. But this Gentile knew Jesus had the power and love to heal from a distance. And because of this man's great faith, because he believed that Jesus can and will do anything, his prayer was answered. At that same hour, the servant was healed. Imagine the officer's joy when he returned home to find the youth as good as new!

Know that Jesus hears your pleas. That your faith in Him can be the tool that connects you to a loved one who needs His healing touch. Keep in mind that your Jesus, the one who is the personification of love, is the one you can count on and has the power to do what you cannot. Be the woman to whom Jesus says, "Because you believed, it has happened."

Lord, when I feel helpless, powerless, I come to You,
requesting Your healing power to help those I cannot reach.

Day 17

Power to Heal (Part 2)

Read John 4:46–54

There was a certain official from the king's court whose son was sick. When he heard that Jesus had come from Judea to Galilee, he went and asked that he come down and heal his son, who was on the brink of death. Jesus put him off: "Unless you people are dazzled by a miracle, you refuse to believe." But the court official wouldn't be put off.

JOHN 4:46–49 MSG

- What signs and wonders has Jesus performed that have helped you to believe in Him?

- A certain nobleman heard Jesus say his son would live, put his trust in that fact, and then went on his way assured it was true. When have you heard Jesus' Word, trusted, and went away assured of His truth? What miracle did you uncover because of that hearing, trust, and assurance?

A government official's son was very sick. Hearing Jesus was in town, he asked him to come and heal his son who lay dying. Jesus tried to put Him off, saying, "You people won't believe Me unless you witness an amazing miracle." But the "official wouldn't be put off." He told Jesus, "Come down!

It's life or death for my son" (John 4:49 MSG).

Jesus responded with "Go home. Your son lives" (John 4:50 MSG). At Jesus' words, the man believed his son would live, so he headed on home. The next day the man's servants met him and told him his son lived! The official asked what time his son began to get better and was told it was about one o'clock the day before. That was the exact time that Jesus claimed the boy lived.

When you are in need of help from Jesus, when you are begging for an answer to prayer, be persistent. Don't allow anything to put you off. Don't just pray one prayer; pray as many as you need. And when you hear Jesus say, "All is well. Your prayer has been answered," take Him at His word. Believe and you will receive.

Lord, I come to You in prayer.
In You I believe! Hear my plea!

Day 18
Loving the Unlovely

Read Luke 5:12–26

A man covered with skin lesions comes along.
As soon as he sees Jesus, he prostrates himself.
Leper: *Lord, if You wish to, You can heal me of my disease.*
Jesus reaches out His hand and touches the man,
something no one would normally do for fear of
being infected or of becoming ritually unclean.
LUKE 5:12–13 VOICE

- Has there ever been a time when you've fallen onto your face, stated your faith, and then simply and humbly awaited Jesus' response and touch? How different is that than just telling Jesus what you want Him to do?

- What do you do, where do you go to recharge spiritually, physically, emotionally, and mentally?

- What do you do when the unlovely, unclean, and undesirable approach? Do you willingly put out your hand and touch them with the love of Jesus? If not, what might help you do so?

There may come a time in your life that you feel unlovely. Perhaps it's an outer condition, a malady that people can plainly see. Or it may be an inner illness—shame, embarrassment, guilt, depression, desperation—that no one can see yet you intensely feel.

Whatever your unloveliness is rooted in or however it may manifest itself, find your way to Jesus. Take your faith and your courage and your humility and throw yourself down at His feet. Tell Him, "Lord, if You wish to, You can heal me."

Then you will find that no matter how gross you feel, Jesus will not turn away from you. He will not recoil in horror. Instead He will reach out His hand and touch you. He will tell you, "I want to heal you," and then do so.

Then, a new woman because Jesus has touched you, you will find yourself unable to hold back your praise! You will feel lovely once more. You may even have a new heart for others who are unlovely in a visible or invisible form. Perhaps then you will find a way to touch the lives of those who need a helping hand, need direction, need a touch from the Master Himself.

Lord, thank You for loving the unlovely. Help me to do the same, to reach out with love to all who need it, no matter their condition within and without.

Day 19
The Cost of Discipleship

Read Mark 8:34–9:1

Calling the crowd to join his disciples, he said, "Anyone who intends to come with me has to let me lead. You're not in the driver's seat; I am. Don't run from suffering; embrace it. Follow me and I'll show you how."

MARK 8:34 MSG

- Do you desire to go after Jesus or shy away from His trail? Do you deny yourself or deny Him? Do you take up your cross or leave it on the ground?

- What does it mean to you when Jesus says that if you want to save your life, you'll lose it; but if you lose your life for Him, you'll save it?

- What might you be putting before God? What might you have gained lately at the expense of your soul?

It's human nature to want to be in charge of your own life, make your own decisions, carve out your own particular niche, and be self-dependent. Yet Jesus has another plan for you. And if you want to follow Him, you must allow Him to have the final say.

That means that you can no longer be the pilot of your own life. Instead, you must allow Jesus that honor, allow Him to be in command.

Some have trouble giving up that control. Though, if you really think about it, Jesus is in command of all—including you—anyway. So why not get in line from the beginning, why not allow Him to lead you where He would have you go? That would save both you and Him a lot of time and energy, wouldn't it?

That's Jesus' message to His followers in today's reading. He wants you to embrace whatever comes your way—good times and bad. And if you follow Him, He will show you exactly how to do that. So if you are wondering what your next move should be in this moment, on this day, in this week, month, year, or life, go ask Jesus. He will help you to get a God-perspective on living on this earth and in the heavenly future to come. He will help you bring out the real you, the woman God designed you to be for this time and place.

Lord, I vow to follow Your lead.
What would You have me do this day?

Day 20
Whᵴ Is thᵴ Greatest?

Read Luke 9:46–62

Then another said, "I'm ready to follow you, Master, but first excuse me while I get things straightened out at home." Jesus said, "No procrastination. No backward looks. You can't put God's kingdom off till tomorrow. Seize the day."

LUKE 9:61–62 MSG

- What are the ways in which you may be seeking to make a name for yourself rather than a name for Jesus?

- When was the last time you steeled yourself to face something difficult? How might what you're learning about Jesus help you in future challenges?

- What steps can you take to keep yourself looking forward instead of backward in your faith walk? What affirming Bible verses might help you in this endeavor?

Remember Lot's wife? After the angels had taken Lot and his family by the hand and led them out of Sodom, they entreated them not to look back. But Lot's wife apparently couldn't resist. She longed to return to her home, to the life she and her family had made for themselves. So she looked back. In so doing, "she turned into a pillar of salt" (Genesis

19:26 NLT), forever stuck where she stood, frozen in time, never to move forward or backward again.

Jesus has given you and all His followers an invitation to allow Him to guide their lives. He begs you not to bemoan your past or have fears and worries about the future. Instead, you are to trust Him to lead you into and through God's kingdom, to seize not just the day but this very moment, to heed His voice and to let everything else fall away, allowing Him to carry you through the day. Are you willing? Will you go? Will you seize this day in Jesus' name? Or will you become forever frozen where you stand, unable to go back or move forward in faith?

Lord, I want to seize the day, to walk Your way, to not look back with regret or fear the future. Help me get there from here.

Day 21
Greatness in the Kingdom

Read Matthew 18

Then he said, "I tell you the truth, unless you turn from your sins and become like little children, you will never get into the Kingdom of Heaven. So anyone who becomes as humble as this little child is the greatest in the Kingdom of Heaven."

MATTHEW 18:3–4 NLT

- Which verse in this chapter struck the loudest chord in your heart? In what ways does that verse connect to/confirm/address the present circumstances of your life?

- How does humbleness play a part in each of the vignettes presented in this chapter? In what ways does this make you stop and take stock of yourself?

- Whom do you find yourself forgiving over and over again? Whom do you need to forgive *from the heart* today?

Today's world urges you to be anything but humble. Some of the highest-rated television shows are contests to see who will be the next idol, the next person propelled to stardom. Some made their career by stepping over people so they could be in the limelight. Some stepped on or overshadowed anyone who got in their way of their spotlight. Some proclaim their aim is to be public servants, when all they really want is to gain and retain power over you. That's exactly the opposite of how and who God wants His people to be.

Jesus implores His followers to be humble, like little children. To accept His leadership absolutely, unquestionably. To go where He would bid them to go, do what He calls them to do without wondering how it would look to other people. Jesus would have His followers forget trying to compete with the Joneses for the nicest house and car, the best career and position.

Jesus' kingdom is much different than the one the world strives for. So look to Him alone. Follow Him alone. Make Him alone your idol.

Help me, Lord, to be as humble as a little child,
looking to serve and follow You alone.

111

Day 22
True Riches

Read Mark 10:13–34

*"Go sell whatever you own and give it to the poor.
All your wealth will then be heavenly wealth.
And come follow me." The man's face clouded over.
This was the last thing he expected to hear, and he
walked off with a heavy heart. He was holding on
tight to a lot of things, and not about to let go.*

MARK 10:21–22 MSG

- In what ways have you accepted Jesus and received the kingdom of God as a little child would? How have you continued to have the unyielding and total faith of a child?

- Where are your treasures residing lately—in heaven or earth? What are those treasures? In answering these questions, what insights are you gleaning about your life?

- In what ways is God giving you the means and motivation to put Him before all earthly treasures? How is He making what seems impossible possible?

We like our stuff. We like to take it with us wherever we go—from home to hotel or missions trip quarters or campground.

Granted, there may be stuff that's attached to cherished memories or is a part of our daily routine. And it gives us comfort to have that stuff around us. But Jesus throws a word of caution in our path in today's reading. He reminds us that nothing we possess should have a hold on us. The only stuff we should be concerned with is the necessities we can use on our walk with Him. All that other stuff, the things we do not need for day-to-day living or to support our families, should all be given to those who don't have.

If you walk into your closet and are holding on to clothes you no longer need or wear, don't keep them from the poor. Donate them. If you have twenty Bibles but only read one, donate some. And if Jesus moves you to give away all you have, do so. For when you follow His lead, when you willingly give to those in need, you'll find your heart so much lighter.

Show me, Lord, what I have that I can give to those who don't have. Give me a heart to offer my riches to the poor.

Day 23
Healing on the Sabbath

Read Luke 13:10–17

*Jesus was teaching in one of the synagogues on the Sabbath.
And there was a woman there who for eighteen years
had had an infirmity caused by a spirit (a demon of
sickness). She was bent completely forward and utterly
unable to straighten herself up or to look upward.*

LUKE 13:10–11 AMPC

- In what ways was Jesus a rebel? In what ways does He *continue* to be a rebel?

- What weight has been bending you over lately? What or who do you need to raise yourself up? What or who do you need to get straight?

- In what instances might you, daughter of Abraham, be blindly following some rules instead of following the promptings of Jesus? What might He be telling you or leading you to?

There was a woman who had been suffering for eighteen years from an illness. She was hunched over, unable to straighten herself or look up. And then she met Jesus.

Even though this woman was bent over for almost two decades, she still got herself up, dressed, and washed and made her way to the temple to meet God. And on one particular day, she met His Son. As soon as He saw her, Jesus called out, "Woman, you're free!" (Luke 13:12 MSG). Then He laid His hands on her and she found herself suddenly standing straight. Finally able to look up, she lifted her eyes and praises to God.

There are some burdens we cannot rid ourselves of. Some have been weighing us down for decades, keeping us from looking up to God with hope. Yet if we remain faithful, if we trust in Jesus, He will see us in the crowd. He will pick up on our malady. He will have the right remedy to heal us, unburden us, straighten us out. And then we too will burst out in praise to the God and His Son who save us.

See me, Lord. Help me. Lift my burden, heal my malady.
I pray You would do for me what I cannot do for myself.

Day 24
Sign of Jonah

Read Matthew 12:22–45

"Every one of these careless words is going to come back to haunt you. There will be a time of Reckoning. Words are powerful; take them seriously. Words can be your salvation. Words can also be your damnation."
MATTHEW 12:36–37 MSG

- What is your fruit? What is it revealing about you to you? To others? To Jesus?

- How are your words saving you? How might they be damning you? How might the fact that your words carry so much power affect your speech in the future? How might that fact affect your thoughts in the future?

- When have you asked God for a sign instead of relying on your faith? What prompted you to do so? What was the result?

Jesus reminds us, "It's your heart, not the dictionary, that gives meaning to your words. A good person produces good deeds and words season after season. An evil person is a blight on the orchard" (Matthew 12:34–35 MSG). Jesus goes on to explain that the words we speak can come back to haunt us. Would that we remember these things every minute of every day.

How many times have you said something that even as the words were coming out of your mouth, you regretted them? How many times have you seen the words you say hurt the hearer? How many times have you been the one hurt by another's careless words?

Children can be especially sensitive to and injured by a loved one's remarks. They can end up carrying those words, nursing the wounds caused by them, into adulthood. And it may be that the speaker of those words has no idea their remarks have had such a biting effect.

Each day, remind yourself that your words have meaning. They have power. They can injure or heal, bring down or lift up, birth heartache or hope. And if the wrong ones emerge, do yourself and the hearer a favor and apologize as soon as you can. For God would have you bearing fruit, not poisoning the orchard.

Lord, help me watch my lips so that I lift up,
not bring down, those who hear my words.

Day 25

Anointing at Bethany

Read Mark 14:1–11

Jesus said, "Let her alone. Why are you giving her a hard time? She has just done something wonderfully significant for me."

MARK 14:6 MSG

- In what ways do you feel like you have done what you could for Jesus? What more might Jesus be prompting you to do for Him?

- When has Jesus prompted you to do something others scorned as a waste of time and money? Did you find yourself responding to Jesus' request or were you swayed into inaction by the naysayers? What was the result?

- How would Jesus have you respond to critics—believers and nonbelievers alike—when you follow through with what God would have you do?

Jesus loves those who love Him with abandon, those who commit themselves wholeheartedly to Him, not caring what others may think or say. Why? Because those people are the ones who see only Him and aspire to serve only Him.

The woman who poured expensive perfume on Jesus' feet was one who loved with abandon. And because of her actions, Jesus told those around them, "You can be sure that wherever in the whole world the Message is preached, what she just did is going to be talked about admiringly" (Mark 14:9 MSG).

There are some who thought the woman pouring perfume on Jesus' feet was ludicrous. They grumbled at her wasting such money. After all, the perfume could've been sold and the money donated to the poor. But that's not the point. This was a woman who followed the promptings of God, inspired to show Jesus how much she loved Him. She did what she could for Jesus—and went all out to do so.

May we be like this woman, doing what we can when we can to love Jesus with abandon, wanting and looking to please Him only.

Help me, Lord, not to worry about what other people may think. For my heart prompts me to go all out in loving You. May I follow its lead rather than that of popular opinion.

Day 26
Institution of the Lord's Supper

Read Mark 14:12–31

Jesus told them, "You're all going to feel that your world is falling apart and that it's my fault. There's a Scripture that says, I will strike the shepherd; the sheep will scatter. But after I am raised up, I will go ahead of you, leading the way to Galilee."
MARK 14:27–28 MSG

- How does it increase your faith knowing that Jesus knows all that is going to greet you in every step of your walk with Him?

- How does the knowledge that Jesus deeply desires you to take communion in remembrance of Him keep the ritual from becoming routine?

- When have you broken a solemn pledge to Jesus—despite your determination to keep it? What does the fact that Jesus not only later forgave Peter but used him greatly to further the kingdom tell you about your Savior?

You may experience days when it feels as if your entire world is falling apart. You look around for someone to blame. And, in some cases, you may want to put a bit of that blame on the God who created you.

On those hard days, you need to remember that even though Jesus specifically told His followers that He was going to be struck down, in a very unpleasant way, He wanted them to have hope that He would be raised up. He wanted them to know He would not desert them. He wanted them to understand that these things had to happen for God's plan to be brought to fruition. Perhaps that's how He was able to sing hymns after the last supper He shared with them.

When you feel as if things couldn't be worse, remember what Jesus suffered. Remember how He always holds out a word of hope for those who follow in His footsteps. Know that He has a "but" in store for you, one that will bring you comfort and give you a greater understanding of who He was and where He is now—going ahead of you, leading the way.

Thank You, Lord, for being my life, my hope,
my comfort. Thank You for going ahead of me,
leading the way. But for You, I would be lost.

Day 27
Betrayal and Arrest of Jesus

Read Luke 22:39–23:25

*He was withdrawn from them about a stone's cast,
and kneeled down, and prayed, saying, Father, if thou
be willing, remove this cup from me: nevertheless
not my will, but thine, be done. And there appeared
an angel unto him from heaven, strengthening him.
And being in an agony he prayed more earnestly.*

LUKE 22:41–44 KJV

- In what ways do you feel you might be following Jesus at a distance? How might that affect how nonbelievers see you? How might it affect you?

- In what situations have you been as meek and quiet as a lamb, knowing that's how God wanted you to be? When have you not been able to contain yourself? What does the fact that Jesus kept His cool reveal about Him?

- When have you gone the way of the crowd instead of the way of God?

At some point, you may experience an arduous situation, one in which the only way out is forward. There is no turning back, for God's will, way, and plan are prodding you on. You know the road ahead will not be easy, but it's the road you are destined to walk.

Jesus experienced the same difficulties. He knew it was His Father's plan that He allow Himself to be mocked, beaten, whipped, and executed. That was the only way that Father God could reconcile His people to Himself. And it was Jesus' cross to bear. So, knowing the only way was forward, Jesus found a spot where, alone, He could pour His heart out to God before facing the inevitable.

Jesus admitted that His upcoming task would be extremely hard to bear. Still, He prayed for God's will to be done, not His. And praying in that way, in line with the will of His Father, God sent an angel from heaven to strengthen Him for the agonizing hours ahead.

When you are facing a difficult situation, go to your Father in prayer. Let Him know you'd be fine with a reprieve but are also more than willing to walk His way, to do His will. Then know He will send you angels to strengthen you for that journey.

Thank You, Lord, for walking with me,
listening to me, and giving me supernatural
strength when the road is difficult.

Day 28
Death of Jesus

Read Matthew 27:33–56

A number of women, who had been devoted to Jesus and followed Him from Galilee, were present, too, watching from a distance. Mary Magdalene was there, and Mary the mother of James and Joseph, and the mother of the sons of Zebedee.

MATTHEW 27:55–56 VOICE

- How do you think Jesus, who had all the power, felt about being presumed and mocked as powerless? Have you ever had the same type of experience?

- When have you been betrayed by a friend, falsely accused, punished, mocked, cursed, and felt God had left you high and dry? How does it feel knowing Jesus suffered all that—and more—*for you*? What does that reveal to you about God? About Jesus?

Jesus' female followers had been sincerely and truly devoted to Him. In their lives, He was the sun, moon, and stars. From the beginning of their meeting Him, they attached themselves to His cause, helped provide for His means, supporting Him as best they could.

And now this dark day has arrived. They stand near His cross, witnessing the scene but separated from Him by the Roman soldiers, unable to provide help, aid, or relief.

We too will have days when we find ourselves unable to help a loved one, when we cannot lift them into our arms, cure their illness, salve their pain, fix their problem. This is especially hard for us as, being female, we are usually more nurturing and compassionate than our counterparts. Yet we can watch. We can pray. We can stand, even if it's far off, and wait patiently to provide whatever comfort we can.

Today, who are you watching from a distance? Who can you pray for? Who needs your comfort? Will you be there for them—if not physically then spiritually?

Lord, give me the patience to help others, even if I must begin by merely standing, watching, waiting from a distance. Give me the words to pray so that my spirit may meld with Yours, connecting me with them. For in You there is no separation from the ones I love.

Day 29
Jesus Is Buried

Read John 19:28–42

And after this, Joseph of Arimathea—a disciple of Jesus, but secretly for fear of the Jews—asked Pilate to let him take away the body of Jesus. And Pilate granted him permission. So he came and took away His body. And Nicodemus also, who first had come to Jesus by night. . .

JOHN 19:38–39 AMPC

- In what ways have you kept your faith in Jesus secret or under cover of darkness for fear of the comments or actions of others? How might it feel to own up to your faith, to step into the light, to take action for Jesus by serving Him before others in some way?

- What do you think about the fact that the Fall of humanity happened in a garden and that the rise of humanity also took place in a garden?

When Jesus was alive, some allowed fear to keep them from publicly following Jesus. They stayed in the shadows during His earthly life, unwilling to acknowledge that they believed He was indeed the Son of God. Yet they finally emerged from the darkness and braved revealing their allegiance to

Jesus in His death.

Joseph of Arimathea came forward first. He girded up his courage and asked Pilate for Jesus' body. What relief he must have felt when his request was granted. Once Joseph had Jesus' physical shell in his possession, Nicodemus also allowed his faith to show. He came bringing myrrh and aloes. Together, Joseph and Nicodemus wrapped Jesus' body in linen cloths and placed it in a new tomb. While Jesus' other disciples had deserted Him in His most trying hour, these two men finally came forward.

Have you dared to let others know how much you love and want to follow Jesus? Have you set your fears aside and boldly claimed Jesus' body of words as your touchstone? Have you courageously emerged from the shadows to do what needs to be done for the Savior you love?

Help me, Lord, to boldly claim my love for You,
Your words as my touchstone, my life as Yours.

Day 30
The Tomb Is Empty

Read John 20:1–18

She turned to leave and saw someone standing there. It was Jesus, but she didn't recognize him. "Dear woman, why are you crying?" Jesus asked her. "Who are you looking for?"

JOHN 20:14–15 NLT

- When was the last time you ran to Jesus, anxious to see the one who calls you "dear woman"? Where do you usually find Him?

- When have you seen—and then believed? In what ways does Jesus bless you for believing in Him even though you have not yet physically seen Him? What helps you keep that faith strong?

- What about the scriptures is still hard for you to understand? What about the scriptures has Jesus made clear to you? What is He revealing to you?

"Dear woman." Can you hear the affection in Jesus' voice?

When you are feeling lost and alone, when you don't know where to find Jesus, when you cannot see Him for the grief and trouble that is clouding your vision, know that Jesus is right there. In all stages and pages of your life, He is closer than you may know. But He is there. And this portion of scripture tells us that.

Mary thought she had lost the one she'd loved. She was searching for some remnant of Him that would remind her that she was not alone. When she could not find Him, she could not help but weep. And how wonderful it must've been when she heard His familiar voice say, "Dear woman, why are you crying?"

Jesus is as close as your breath. He is nearer than your heart. He is living and breathing and aching for you to see Him. Today, open your eyes. See Jesus before you. Feel the solace of His presence. Feel the light that warms your very spirit as His envelops your own.

Lord, open my eyes so that I may see You, my spirit so that I may hear You, my heart so that I may know You. Today and forevermore. Amen.

30 Days of Bible Readings for Growing in Your Faith

It was by faith that Abraham obeyed when God called him to leave home and go to another land that God would give him as his inheritance. He went without knowing where he was going.

HEBREWS 11:8 NLT

The more you grow your faith, the stronger your relationship with God will become. The stronger your relationship, the more in tune you will be with the one who will lead you to wonderful places, places you never dreamed or began to imagine. The more courage you will have to walk where He wants you to walk, to do what He has called you to do. And you will find yourself doing it with ease and peace of mind and heart.

The great adventure begins and ends in the Word. In the next 30 days, you will be growing your faith by soaking in God's truth, allowing it to become a part of your very being. Soon, you will find yourself being prompted, actuated, and urged on by faith, waiting confidently and looking expectantly for what God will have you do next.

Approach the Word with reverence, read the scripture, intend to hear God speak and the Spirit translate. Meditate upon what you've read, underline the passage that stands out the most. Then read and reflect upon the questions from that day's reading. Afterward, read that day's devotion and pray, knowing God will lead you in your walk of faith.

Day 1
Faith: Trusting God with Everything

Read Genesis 22:1–14

Abraham named the place Yahweh-Yireh (which means "the LORD will provide"). To this day, people still use that name as a proverb: "On the mountain of the LORD it will be provided."

GENESIS 22:14 NLT

- When have you obeyed God without question or hesitation? What was at stake? How did that experience confirm and strengthen your faith?

- When has God provided *for* you when you offered that which He demanded *from* you? How did that grow your faith and trust in Him?

- What current situation in your life is testing your faith and obedience to God? What do you feel you may have to sacrifice?

When God called Abraham to leave his home, he didn't hesitate (Hebrews 11:8). Not once. Even though he had no idea where he was going, "Abram departed, as the LORD had spoken unto him" (Genesis 12:4 KJV). And he did so at the age of seventy-five.

Because Abraham had faith in God, he believed His promise. He believed that God would be with him, lead him, and not only bless him but make him a blessing (Genesis 12:2). And God did.

Thus, when God told Abraham to sacrifice and offer up to Him his son—Isaac, Abraham's one and only son, the one God had promised him and he had waited years to see manifested in his life—Abraham took Isaac, the fire, and the wood, and he went.

Just as Abraham had the knife in his hand and was ready to plunge it into Isaac's body, God not only stayed his hand but offered him a substitute sacrifice, a ram caught in a thicket (Genesis 22:10, 13). Abraham had once proven his faith to God by leaving home for an unknown destination. Now he proved how much he respected and feared God, holding back nothing from what God asked of him.

Just as God supplied all for Abraham, He will supply all for you. Walk strong in that faith, knowing God will always provide and prove His promises.

Help me, Lord, to understand and believe with all my heart that You will always be true to Your promises and provide all I could ever need or want.

Day 2
Faith: Trusting God through Prayer

Read 1 Samuel 1:7–20

[Hannah] was in distress of soul, praying to the Lord and weeping bitterly. . . . Hannah was speaking in her heart; only her lips moved but her voice was not heard.

1 SAMUEL 1:10, 13 AMPC

- When have you gone to the Lord with a broken heart, crying bitter tears and pouring out your soul to Him in prayer, trusting in His compassion? How did you feel afterward?

- Have you kept the vows you have made to God, being faithful to the part you have promised to play in your relationship with Him?

- How do you prayerfully approach God—from the heart or from the head? Do you rise with a peaceful or preoccupied countenance?

Not yet birthing a child, Hannah was teased, ridiculed, and harassed by her husband's fertile and peevish second wife, Peninnah. In anguish, Hannah went to the Lord on her knees and poured out her heart and soul in prayer. Through her tears, Hannah asked that the Lord provide her with a son. In exchange, she would offer that son right back to the Lord. God answered her plea, enabling Hannah to birth Samuel, the priest, prophet, and judge that would later anoint kings. God kept His side of the bargain and Hannah hers.

Corrie ten Boom once said, "A man is powerful on his knees." The same holds true for women. Corrie not only helped her family hide Jews during World War II but was later imprisoned in a concentration camp. Through it all, she continued to study the Word, pray on her knees, stay strong in her faith, and survive the horrors of the Nazi regime, eventually becoming a Christian writer and speaker.

Follow the examples of the women who have gone before you, praying their hearts out on their knees. Allow the fact that God sees your anguish and hears your heartfelt prayers to buoy your spirit. Grow your faith knowing He will remain devoted to you in the same measure you are devoted to Him.

Down on my knees, I pour out my prayer, Lord.
I then rise composed, at peace, knowing You've heard my
words, confident You will answer my plea. Thank You, Lord,
for being so faithful to me. May I be as faithful to You.

Day 3
Faith: Trusting God for Protection

Read 2 Chronicles 20:20–30

Jehoshaphat: *Listen to me, Judah and inhabitants of Jerusalem. Trust in the Eternal One, your True God, not in your own abilities, and you will be supported. Put your trust in His words that you heard through the prophets, and we will succeed.*

2 CHRONICLES 20:20 VOICE

- In difficult circumstances, you may find yourself looking around instead of up. What can you do to keep your eyes focused on your heavenly God?

- When have you sung praises to God, confident He would look out for, protect, and bless you, in the midst of a seemingly hopeless and potentially dangerous situation? How did that attitude and outlook help see you through?

- What do you have to sing praises to God about today?

Jehoshaphat, the king of Judah, had heard that three armies were coming against him and his people. So he got down on his knees and prayed, "We don't know what to do, but our eyes are on You, Lord" (2 Chronicles 20:12).

God then answered through one of His prophets, "Be not afraid nor dismayed by. . .this great multitude; for the battle is not yours, but God's. . . . Ye shall not need to fight in this battle: set yourselves, stand ye still, and see the salvation of the LORD" (2 Chronicles 20:15, 17 KJV). And the king and his people took God at His word.

The next day, Jehoshaphat sent the singers out before his army. As they began praising God in song, He moved the enemy armies to turn against each other. Not one man was left alive, leaving Jehoshaphat and his people to simply collect the spoils their enemies had left behind.

You too can allow your faith to lead you out of trouble and into victory. It simply takes a humble heart, being willing to get down on your knees and beg for God's help, admitting that you don't know what to do but you have your eyes on the Lord of your life. Take His Word as fact and then simply praise Him, knowing His blessings will follow!

Lord, I have no idea what to do, but my eyes are on You, and my complete faith is in You!

Day 4
Faith: Trusting God to the End

Read Daniel 3

"I see four men, walking around freely in the fire,
completely unharmed! And the fourth man looks
like a son of the gods!" . . . "Blessed be the God of
Shadrach, Meshach, and Abednego! He sent his angel
and rescued his servants who trusted in him!"

DANIEL 3:25, 28 MSG

- What false idol might you have trusted and worshipped more than God? What came of this misdirected faith and adoration?

- When have you proclaimed you would have faith and trust in God, worshipping and serving Him—regardless of whether or not He saved you from an undesirable end?

- God walks with you amid fiery situations, keeping you unsinged spiritually, physically, emotionally, mentally, or financially. How does that truth grow your faith even more?

Shadrach, Meshach, and Abednego were exiled Jews living in Babylon. They refused to bow down and worship a gold statue that King Nebuchadnezzar had erected. When their disrespect to this icon had been reported to the king, he questioned the men.

The trio said the king's threats were nothing to them. They continued: "If you throw us in the fire, the God we serve can rescue us from your roaring furnace and anything else you might cook up, O king. But even if he doesn't, it wouldn't make a bit of difference, O king. We still wouldn't serve your gods or worship the gold statue you set up" (Daniel 3:17–18 MSG).

So the irate Nebuchadnezzar had them thrown into the furnace. Soon after, he noticed a "son of the gods" walking in the flames with them. When the king ordered them out, Shadrach, Meshach, and Abednego were not only not singed—they didn't even smell of smoke!

The God you belong to will be with you no matter where you go. He'll be with you through the fires and the floods. All you need to do is trust in Him, no matter what threat you face. When you do, angels—seen and unseen—will be by your side.

Lord, I trust in You alone. I worship You alone.
For You have promised to walk by my side, no matter
how deep the water or how hot the flames.

Day 5
Faith in His Power

Read Matthew 8:1–13; 15:21–28

*A man with leprosy approached him and knelt
before him. "Lord," the man said, "if you are willing,
you can heal me and make me clean." Jesus reached
out and touched him. "I am willing," he said. "Be
healed!" And instantly the leprosy disappeared.*

MATTHEW 8:2–3 NLT

- Have you, while worshipping Jesus, told Him that, if He is willing, He *has* the power to heal you? How might this be more of a faith booster than telling Him *how* you'd like Him to heal you?

- Jesus' healing touch can reach beyond time and distance. How has that proven true in your life or the lives of those you love?

- How persistent are you in crying out to Jesus, worshipping Him, requesting He heal someone you love? How has doing so changed you?

Jesus has some amazing powers, the greatest of which is His eternal love for you. Because of that eternal love, He is more than willing and able to heal you. The question is, have you asked Him to heal you, or have you suggested how He do so?

The leper came to Jesus, knowing where he'd find Him—just as He was coming down a mountainside. He humbly "dropped to his knees before Jesus, praying" (Matthew 8:2 MSG). Still on his knees, most likely with his head bowed, his heart and spirit in full worship of the Son of God before him, the leper made a statement of faith: "If you are willing, you can heal me and make me clean" (Matthew 8:2 NLT). There was no doubt in this poor man's mind that Jesus had the power to do what no one else could do. So Jesus simply reached out, touched him, admitted He was willing, and commanded he be healed—and the man's leprosy vanished.

You can do the same. Know that Jesus loves and cares for you. That He has the power to heal you. All you need to do is meet Him where He's at. Humble yourself before Him, worship Him, and clearly make a statement of faith, acknowledging that He has the power to heal you. Know He will reach out and respond. He could not do otherwise.

Lord, I humbly seek Your presence.
If You are willing, You can heal me.

141

Day 6
Faith in Touch

Read Matthew 9:18–31; 14:34–36

Behold, a woman who had suffered from a flow of blood for twelve years came up behind Him and touched the fringe of His garment; for she kept saying to herself, If I only touch His garment, I shall be restored to health.

MATTHEW 9:20–21 AMPC

- When has your persistent, doggedly determined, against-all-odds faith prompted you to reach out to touch Jesus and made you well—spiritually, physically, emotionally, or mentally?

- What happens to you if your life is dependent upon the faith you have in Jesus' abilities and power to touch and change you and, at times, your circumstances? What proof have you seen of this in your life?

- What touch do you need from Jesus today?

Imagine hemorrhaging blood for twelve years. You've spent all your money on doctors who haven't helped you one iota. Then you hear accounts about a man who has successfully healed other people. And you begin to believe. Then you begin to plan.

Even though you know you would be considered dirty and untouchable to the crowd around you, you decide to seek out this man, this Jesus. You keep saying to yourself, "If I can just touch His robe, I'll be cured. . . . If I can just touch His robe, I'll be cured. . . . If I can just touch His robe, I'll be cured. . . ." The constant repetition of this statement of faith spurs you on, motivates you to continue on this healing quest.

The moment comes. You see Jesus amid the people. You approach Him. You continue your mantra as you reach out and touch Him. Suddenly Jesus stops. He turns. You tremble. And then you hear Him say, "Take heart, daughter. Your faith has healed you" (Matthew 9:22 VOICE). And you feel the bleeding stop. From that moment you are healed. Your world is forever changed. One touch and you are whole.

Take the faith you have. Reach out to Jesus. Connect with Him, knowing He has the power to help you in whatever way you need. Know that He can and will heal you—with one touch.

I take heart, Lord, knowing that my faith can heal me.
I reach out for You now, Jesus, longing to connect.

Day 7
Faith in Action

Read Matthew 17:14–20; 21:18–22

I tell you this: if you have faith and do not doubt, then you will be able to wither a fig tree with one glance. You will be able to tell mountains to throw themselves into the ocean, and they will obey. If you believe, whatever you ask for in prayer will be granted.

MATTHEW 21:21–22 VOICE

- When have your needs and desperation driven you to your knees before Jesus? What remedy did you request? What part did your faith play?

- Regardless of your amount of faith in a particular area or circumstance, all things are possible with God. How has that fact boosted your faith enough to take action against all odds?

- In what areas of your life do your doubts erode your faith? What can you do to shore up that faith?

"If you believe, whatever you ask for in prayer will be granted." That's all it takes. That's what Jesus tells you. If you have faith, the impossible is possible. Why? Because God is in it with you.

That's the key. Going to God, giving Him the problem, challenge, obstacle, and believing that He has a solution. That He in His time is going to fix the problem, meet the challenge, and remove the mountain of an obstacle that stands before you, impeding your progress. All you have to do is believe.

Yet there is another thing to keep in mind, not to take away from your faith but to put it into God's perspective. You will have an answer if you have faith, if you pray. But it may not be the answer you thought you'd get, and it may not come according to your timetable. That's because whatever happens in your life must be according to God's plan for you, not *your* plan for you.

As writer and preacher A. W. Tozer said, "To pray effectively we must want what God wants—that and that only is to pray in the will of God."

Lord, teach me how to pray, to put my
faith and Your will in action.

Day 8
Faith Grows

Read Isaiah 40:27–31; Mark 10:13–16

*Those who wait for the Lord [who expect, look for, and
hope in Him] shall change and renew their strength and
power; they shall lift their wings and mount up [close to
God] as eagles [mount up to the sun]; they shall run and not
be weary, they shall walk and not faint or become tired.*

ISAIAH 40:31 AMPC

- In what ways do you nourish your fledgling faith so that
  it cannot just grow but take flight? What role does God,
  Jesus, and the Holy Spirit play in your spiritual nurturing?

- How do you wait upon the Lord with confidence and
  hopeful expectation? How does doing so increase strength
  you may not realize you have?

- God would rather you approach Him like a divine child to
  a heavenly father than a petitioner to an authority figure.
  Which is rooted in love? Which is more effective?

Need some more energy? Some strength? A break from the
rat race?

Look up. Expect God to move in your life, to be working
in it. Know that His good plan for you is already in motion.

Look for Him wherever you go, whatever you're doing. Even in the least likely of places, you will find Him. Keep your hope in Him. For He is the one who hovered over the deep, dark waters and brought in a light that darkness can never ever, ever dispel.

Sit tight and walk tall, knowing that when you wait for God, when you trust in Him with all your heart, soul, mind, and strength, He will move. How? He'll transform you into the woman He created you to be. He'll give you a major boost in your strength and power. Next thing you know, you'll be flying so high in faith that you will become closer to God than you ever imagined possible. You'll feel the warmth of His breath on your face, the touch of His hand upon your own. Then you will no longer tire. You'll be able to walk the distance, fully following Him to heavenly heights.

Here I am, Lord, waiting, looking, trusting in You alone. Rising up into Your presence, I find the energy I have longed for, energy that will keep me following hard after You.

Day 9
Faith in God's Glory

Read John 7:38–39; 20:24–31

*Jesus provided far more God-revealing signs than are
written down in this book. These are written down
so you will believe that Jesus is the Messiah, the Son
of God, and in the act of believing, have real and
eternal life in the way he personally revealed it.*

JOHN 20:30–31 MSG

- Through Jesus, God provides supernatural water for spiritually parched people. In what ways do you thirst for God? How do you satisfy that thirst?

- Once relieved of spiritual thirst, are you a refreshing conduit of the Holy Spirit, allowing His rejuvenating waters to flow through you and onto others?

- In what areas of your life do you give more weight and credence to what you can see rather than what you believe? How might Jesus be prompting you to believe and be blessed?

In his Gospel accounts, John includes many signs that Jesus performed. But not all. John just recorded enough so that people born after Jesus and the disciples could understand who He was and what they could have access to if they only believed. This begs readers to imagine all the miracles that Jesus has performed in the lives of believers who lived when He lived and were born after His death!

We have truly no idea all the actions Jesus took, all the lessons He taught, all the messages He preached, nor all the miracles He wrought when He was walking among God's children. As John later writes, "There are so many other things Jesus did. If they were all written down, each of them, one by one, I can't imagine a world big enough to hold such a library of books" (John 21:25 MSG).

All Jesus' followers need to do is believe. And when you believe, when you trust that Jesus is the Son of God, that the world was created through Him, that you are forgiven because of Him, that you can do the impossible through Him, anything can happen. All to His glory and your joy.

You, Lord, satisfy me in so many ways. Work through me now as I walk through this world, with faith in Your glory and a solid belief in Your miracle-wielding Son.

149

Day 10
Faith Is Intentional

Read Romans 10:17–21; 2 Corinthians 5:6–7

People found and welcomed me who never so much as looked for me. And I found and welcomed people who had never even asked about me. . . . Day after day after day, I beckoned Israel with open arms, and got nothing for my trouble but cold shoulders and icy stares.

Romans 10:20–21 MSG

- When God's message is heard, faith grows. Are you intentionally listening to God when He speaks, or are you distracted by the noise of the world?

- In what ways might God be stretching out His hands to you, but you, not even looking for Him, cannot see them?

- How might your life change and your faith grow if you intentionally sought God's face and presence? What if you listened alertly, were all ears, waiting for Him to speak, to understand His words and meaning?

There's nothing more annoying than when you are talking to someone, her eyes glaze over at some point, and you know you've lost her. When you end your monologue with a question, she suddenly comes back alive, saying, "Sorry. I just drifted off there. . . . What were you saying?"

Even worse is when someone you want to reach or help just turns and walks away.

That's how God felt with the Israelites. He'd opened His arms to them, waiting for them to come running to Him, to feel His love and secure His protection. But they simply turned away. So He says He has been discovered by "those who did not seek Me; I have shown (revealed) Myself to those who did not [consciously] ask for Me" (Romans 10:20 AMPC).

God is reaching out for you, wanting you to come to Him, to become a part of His world. He wants to help you become the woman He created you to be. He wants you to understand Him, to love Him, to open your eyes, ears, heart, and spirit to His own.

Today, take an intentional step toward God. Take in what He is ready to pour out over you.

Thank You, Lord, for longing for me to be a part of Your world, every moment of the day. I open my eyes, ears, heart, mind, and spirit to Your call.

Day 11
Faith through Your Doubts

Read Galatians 3:1–14

Does God give you the Holy Spirit and work miracles among you because you obey the law? Of course not! It is because you believe the message you heard about Christ. In the same way, "Abraham believed God, and God counted him as righteous because of his faith." The real children of Abraham, then, are those who put their faith in God.

GALATIANS 3:5–7 NLT

- Spiritual strength is more pleasing to God than human effort. Do you strain to please Him through physical works or by soaking in His Word, coming to Him in prayer, allowing His Spirit to fill you, following wherever He leads?

- How do you keep the gospel fresh in your mind and a cornerstone of faith? How does that stave off any doubts that might creep in?

- Are you a daughter of Abraham, trusting and relying on God, stepping out even though you don't know what lies ahead?

God has a system. He's made it simple. You need not try to obey the laws to be made right. All you need to do is believe.

That's it. Done deal!

That's how it worked for Abraham (then called Abram). He "believed in (trusted in, relied on, remained steadfast to) the Lord" (Genesis 15:6 AMPC). And because he did so, "God declared him 'Set-Right-with-God'" (Genesis 15:6 MSG).

God had come to Abraham in a vision and told him to fear nothing. That He would be his shield and protector. That Abraham would be rewarded for his loyalty to God. That this childless man would be the father of many nations. And because Abraham believed God, had full confidence that what He promised would become manifested in Abraham's life, God called him "Set-Right-with-God."

You have the same opportunity as Abraham had. All you need to do is believe in God, stick close to Him, sure that His promises will become your reality, and you will be right with God.

Open your eyes and take a look at your life. If you find that in some areas you are straining to please God through human efforts, stop. Start trusting God, relying on Him, remaining committed to Him in all ways, and you will be called "Set-Right-with God."

I believe in and trust You alone, Lord, with all I am, have, and hope to be. Thank You for allowing me to be right with You through faith alone!

Day 12
Faith despite the Fight

Read Philippians 3:7–11

Compared to the high privilege of knowing Christ Jesus as my Master, firsthand, everything I once thought I had going for me is insignificant—dog dung. I've dumped it all in the trash so that I could embrace Christ and be embraced by him.

PHILIPPIANS 3:8 MSG

- Faith changes your values. What in your life is becoming increasingly less important as you continue your faith walk? What has become more important?

- What are you striving for—following a bunch of holy rules or getting to know Christ intimately? Which makes you stronger and fiercer in your spiritual journey?

- What might it feel like to get so close to Christ that you experience His resurrection power? How close are you to doing so?

When we find Christ, it's amazing how many things we once thought were so important lose their value. For if we allow Him to, He can change our world. Others, those who don't know Christ, may be bothered by this. They may wonder what has happened to us, the women they once knew—or thought they knew. They may try to get us back into their fold.

It may be hard for us to describe what we have found when we are trusting in and continually seeking Christ. All we really know is that He is the better part of us. He is the one who promises to and does transform us into the women He created us to be. Each time we find out something more about Him, we grow closer and closer to His light. In a strange way, it is almost like coming home.

When you feel as if you are being pulled back into your old life, remember who you are in Christ. Remember who He has become to you. Don't go digging in the trash for who you used to be just to please others. Instead, continually lean into Christ. For how much sweeter it is to embrace Him and to be embraced by Him. With Him in your life, you've never been richer.

Thank You, Lord, for changing my life,
for transforming my soul, for speaking to my
spirit. In Jesus' name I pray. Amen.

Day 13
Faith to Approach God

Read Hebrews 4:16; 10:19–25

Let us then fearlessly and confidently and boldly draw near to the throne of grace (the throne of God's unmerited favor to us sinners), that we may receive mercy [for our failures] and find grace to help in good time for every need [appropriate help and well-timed help, coming just when we need it].

HEBREWS 4:16 AMPC

- Jesus has been through it all and seen it all. How does that knowledge give you the boldness to walk right up to Him and ask for help, understanding, and compassion? What else are you in need of that He is more than ready to give?

- Now that Jesus has opened the doorway to God, how confident are you that you are presentable to Him? That He will keep His promises and never go back on His Word?

How easy it is to get caught up in the world's doings and machinations, forgetting that all the help, grace, and wisdom we need are found in God. How quickly we can move out of our devotions and into our day, thinking that we are on our own, that it is our energy, our strength, our wisdom, our power that will get us through the hours ahead.

Jesus has been through and seen it all. He has been rejected and tested and experienced more than we may in our own lifetime. Yet He came through it all with flying colors. Not once did He sin in the eyes of God. Yet He also went to God, communicating with Him through morning and evening prayer. When feeding others, He asked God to bless the food. When healing others, He looked up to heaven for help. When going through the hardest of times, He called on God, who would send Him angels to give Him strength.

Jesus is the example we are to follow. Would that we would keep that in mind every moment of our day, going through Him to God for forgiveness, for strength in time of need, for mercy when we mess up, for grace in all ways, and for help that arrives just in the nick of time.

Lord, I approach Your throne, looking for
what You are ready, able, and willing to give
as I walk through this life in You.

Day 14
Faith in Our Future Home

Read Hebrews 11

*Faith is the assurance of things you have hoped for,
the absolute conviction that there are realities you've
never seen. . . . Without faith no one can please God
because the one coming to God must believe He
exists, and He rewards those who come seeking.*

HEBREWS 11:1, 6 VOICE

- When your Creator God spoke, He made visible things appear out of the invisible. In what ways does God's Word continue to fashion your world?

- The Bible contains amazing examples of historical faith walkers. How does this list boost your faith? Who do you most identify with?

- In what ways do invisible things—such as air and gravity—confirm your belief in God, Jesus, and the Holy Spirit? How do you draw near to an invisible God? How does He reward you, an earnest and diligent seeker?

Women of faith have walked before you. Absolutely convinced of God and His powers, they leaned into His promises, took them up as solid truths, facts to be relied on. And because of their faith, they were rewarded.

Consider the barren Sarah, married to Abraham to whom God had promised many descendants. She'd tried to come up with her own solution. But in the end, she hung on to her faith and became pregnant at a very old age because "she believed that God would keep his promise" (Hebrews 11:11 NLT). Consider Jochebed who had the faith to defy the king's edict, hiding her child and then setting him in an ark in the Nile, knowing God would take care of her beautiful baby Moses (Hebrews 11:23). Consider Rahab who welcomed God's spies into Jericho, knowing their God was more powerful than any other (Hebrews 11:31) and later became the great-grandmother of King David, an ancestor of Jesus.

Consider all those who have gone before you in the Old Testament and New. Have faith in God, knowing you are on the road to rewards in Him and the home to which He will call you.

Lord, in You alone I have faith. I come seeking You, longing for Your presence, knowing that with You time stands still and that eventually You will lead me to my eternal home.

Day 15
Faith Drives Good Works

Read James 2:14–26

We are made right with God through good works, not simply by what we believe or think. Even Rahab the prostitute was made right with God by hiding the spies and aiding in their escape. Removing action from faith is like removing breath from a body. All you have left is a corpse.

JAMES 2:24–26 VOICE

- Your faith is revealed by your actions. What good works does your faith prompt you to perform? How are you satisfying those urgings? Have you asked God to approve the work of your hands?

- Who can you help today? What actions can you take to alleviate someone's suffering, directly or indirectly, openly or covertly?

- How are your actions, your works, making your faith complete? How are your works alone showing others you are right with God?

It's inspiring to hear people give their testimony of faith. You marvel at how much courage they had to stand up and tell others what God has done in their lives. They even seem to

160

be able to recite appropriate Bible passages. But later you might see those same people walking by a collection box for the poor or not signing up for any work that needs to be done at the church.

Granted, we have no idea what people do in their private lives. And it's really not our place to judge. But we do know what we ourselves are doing—or not doing—as far as good works are concerned.

Imagine if Rahab genuinely believed in God but then turned in the spies Joshua had sent to reconnoiter Jericho. Imagine if Ruth had believed in God but then ditched her mother-in-law Naomi, leaving her to fend for herself.

God wants your faith to be backed up by your actions. Each day, ask Him to steer you toward any area where your help and compassion may be needed. Put some feet to your faith, and you will be awed at where God takes you!

Help me, Lord, put some feet to my faith. Who would You have me help today? How about tomorrow?

Day 16
Faith in the Spirit

Read John 15:26–16:15; 1 John 3:21–24

I am telling you nothing but the truth when I say it is profitable. . .for you that I go away. Because if I do not go away, the Comforter (Counselor, Helper, Advocate, Intercessor, Strengthener, Standby) will not come to you [into close fellowship with you]; but if I go away, I will send Him to you [to be in close fellowship with you].

JOHN 16:7 AMPC

- Jesus left behind the Holy Spirit to help you live, love, and serve God and His people. What words of praise do you have for the Helper and Comforter?

- How is the Holy Spirit guiding you? What truths is He revealing to you?

- Which of the Holy Spirit's roles—Comforter, Counselor, Strengthener, Standby, Advocate, Intercessor, etc.—is He playing most predominantly in your life right now?

Some days you may feel as if everything and everyone are against you. That's when you need to remember you are not walking through your life alone. The Holy Spirit is available to help you take on any challenge that comes your way, to overcome any obstacle in your path.

Some call the Holy Spirit the Comforter, for He can raise you up when you are down. He's also known as the Counselor, ready to bring you whatever wisdom you need when you need it. Some call Him the Advocate or Intercessor, for He will plead with the Father on your behalf. Others think of Him as the Strengthener, giving them the energy they need to power through things when they can barely lift their heads. And some view the Spirit as the Standby, always there when you need Him, twenty-four hours a day, seven days a week.

When you're discouraged over the things that happen or don't happen in your life, turn to the Holy Spirit. Know that He will never disappoint and is always there to help you, in whatever shape or form you need it.

Jesus, thank You so much for leaving me the Holy Spirit, my all in all. Because of Him and You, my faith is rewarded over and over again!

Day 17

Faith in the Final Outcome

Read 1 John 5:1–12

*And this is the truth: God has given us the gift of
eternal life, and this life is in His Son. If you have
the Son, you have eternal life. If you do not have the
Son of God, you are not acquainted with true life.*

1 JOHN 5:11–12 VOICE

- Jesus' sacrifice entitles you to eternal life with God. How is He, your ultimate Savior, showing up in your life?

- As a believer in Jesus, you are considered born of God, *and* your faith gives you victory over the world. In what ways are you, daughter of God, triumphing in your life?

- How does your perspective change when you realize that because of your faith in Jesus you are already living the life eternal?

God is your Creator and Father who has fashioned you in love and light. As His child, you are not just to love all of your fellow brothers and sisters but to walk in the light of Christ. And this is just the beginning.

You, sister in Christ, are in your mere infancy. Once your earth suit is no longer viable, you will be winging your way with God in some other form. Just another step on the road to eternity promised in God.

When you look at this world and your place in it from an eternal perspective, everything changes. The little things that drive you crazy become less important and irritating. You begin to see things with God's point of view. In Him, love and light overwhelm, dissipating fear and doubt. You are filled with an overwhelming peace. Deep within you realize all is well and all will always be well because you follow the one who tames the chaos with His light, calming all within its radiant reach.

Each morning, before you get caught up in the busyness of your day, remember that you, a precious and well-loved daughter of God and sister of Christ, are living an eternal life. Take a moment to allow His peace to calm your chaos, His light to extinguish your darkness, His name to carry you home.

Thank You, Lord, for the eternal love, light, and life You have blessed me with. May I view each day with Your timeless perspective.

Day 18
Obedience to His Commandments

Read 1 John 2:3–6; 2 John 6–9

He who keeps (treasures) His Word [who bears in
mind His precepts, who observes His message in its
entirety], truly in him has the love of and for God
been perfected (completed, reached maturity).

1 JOHN 2:5 AMPC

- Who do you think Jesus may have found difficult to love? Who do *you* find it difficult to love? In what ways can you love that person with the love of Jesus?

- Jesus commands you to love and to walk as He walked. How does your doing so not only grow your faith but also demonstrate your love for Him?

- How does your staying faithful to the teachings of Christ keep you closely tied to both Christ your Brother and God your Father?

What happens when you open your Bible? Do you do so with great anticipation or as just one more obligation to fulfill?

Those who are truly God's followers will treasure all the wisdom contained in the Word from Genesis to Revelation.

God's followers are eager to write His words upon their hearts. For then they will be able to apply them to their lives, live out His message to the world.

Jesus' main message is one of love. His two greatest commandments are to love God with all your heart, soul, mind, and strength and to love others as you love yourself. That sounds like a tall order. But the more you attempt to live in that love and to shower it upon God, yourself, and others, the more lovely this world will be and the more you will look and act like Jesus.

The Word is your road map to not just surviving on this earthly plane but doing so with the intention of living, loving, and walking in the light of Christ. Today as you dip into the Word, do so with all your heart, mind, soul, and strength. Respond to it. Obey it. Love it. Walk as Jesus walked. And your intimacy with Him will grow greater and greater.

Lord of love and light, lead me into Your Word. Show me what You would have me write upon my heart and mind. Then help me walk as You walked, love as You loved, live as You lived.

167

Day 19
Obedience Trumps Sacrifice

Read 1 Samuel 15:12–23

Does the Eternal One delight in sacrifices and burnt offerings as much as in perfect obedience to His voice? Be certain of this: that obedience is better than sacrifice; to heed His voice is better than offering the fat of rams.

1 SAMUEL 15:22 VOICE

- When have you prided yourself on following God's promptings only to later realize you'd fallen short of all He'd wanted you to do?

- Why might you only hear (or listen to) half of what God says? What can you do to ensure you're giving God your total attention so that you can be wholly obedient?

- God views your obedience and submission as being more valuable to Him than any sacrifice or offering you could make. Where do you need to obey and submit to Him today?

King Saul was in deep trouble. God had told him to fight off all of the Amalekites until they, as well as everything they possessed, were completely destroyed. But instead of obeying God, "Saul and the army spared Agag, and they saved. . .the best of all the stock. They kept what was valuable instead of destroying it, and they only destroyed those things they considered worthless" (1 Samuel 15:9 VOICE).

God came and spoke to Samuel the priest, telling him that Saul had not followed His commands. The Lord regretted ever making Saul king over His people Israel. The next morning, Samuel caught up with Saul, who had built a monument honoring himself, planning on sacrificing to God the best of the Amalekites' stock later that day. Samuel told Saul that since Saul had rejected God, God was now rejecting Saul as king over His people.

When we think we know more than God and so reject His wisdom, His Word, His edicts, His commands and follow our own, we're heading for trouble. It's our obedience God is after, not our own bright ideas. For nothing is more resplendent than God's wisdom.

Lord, help me to submit to Your commands, Your words, Your wisdom. Help me turn all my attention to Your voice so that I may walk in Your way every day.

169

Day 20
Obedience Honors His Holiness

Read Psalm 119:1–10

*You're blessed when you stay on course, walking
steadily on the road revealed by GOD. You're blessed
when you follow his directions, doing your best to
find him. That's right—you don't go off on your
own; you walk straight along the road he set.*

PSALM 119:1–3 MSG

- Your obedience to God's will, Word, and way keeps you on the *right*eous track. How does such submission result in your joy and God's pleasure?

- How can you keep your whole heart seeking after God? What can you do to keep your spiritual appetite whetted and nourished?

- When might you have felt you were far from where God wants you to be? What in God's Word inspires you to keep on following Him, to celebrate faith-walk milestones?

In your house or perhaps in your hands at this very moment, you have a guide to life at your fingertips. It's called the Bible. Within it you will find all you need to know to keep yourself on the right road, walking the way God would have you walk.

God doesn't want you to wander off on your own. When you do, chances are good that you'll veer off in the wrong direction. God has prescribed the way He wants you to live. Now He expects you to follow that prescription.

Nothing can fill you with regret more than stumbling off the straight and narrow. So, to keep your whole heart seeking after God, consider reading a new devotional, something that will give you a new perspective on what God would have you do, how He would have you live. Or consider investing in a new Bible translation, one that would whet your appetite for God's Word, spurring you to feed on it morning, noon, and night.

God loves when His daughters are on the same page as He is. So take steps today to dig into God's Word more than ever before so that you'll be sure to stay close to Him, walking in His footsteps day after day.

Give me a new perspective on Your Word,
Lord, so that I will be walking on the road You
have revealed with every step I take.

Day 21
Obedience Leads to Righteousness

Read Deuteronomy 6; Romans 2:1–16

And you shall love the Lord your God with all your [mind and] heart and with your entire being and with all your might. And these words which I am commanding you this day shall be [first] in your [own] minds and hearts.

DEUTERONOMY 6:5–6 AMPC

- In what ways does obeying God's commands and worshipping *only Him* keep you in the land flowing with milk and honey?

- Snuggle up to God, telling Him you love Him with all your heart, soul, and strength. Record your thoughts and feelings. How might practicing this exercise keep you on the right path with God—and lead others to follow?

- How does recalling all God has done for you keep your faith strong and your walk sure?

God wants you to love Him with all you are and all you have. Why? "For [your] good always, that He might preserve" you (Deuteronomy 6:24 AMPC). That's why!

When you are following the course God has set out for you, when you follow His precepts and obey Him, when you run to Him for refuge, help, support, and strength, when you seek Him for encouragement, when you make Him your all in all, you'll be not just on the right path but in the right place—a loving place, where you and God are entwined in heart, spirit, and mind.

God makes it clear that "if you embrace the way God does things, there are wonderful payoffs, again without regard to where you are from or how you were brought up" (Romans 2:10 MSG). And what do those payoffs include? Peace of mind and heart.

Obeying God in all ways doesn't mean that you'll stop being you. You'll always be special in His eyes. But what it does mean is that you'll become more and more like the woman He created you to be.

Lord, I love You more than life itself. Now please show me each and every day what You would have me do, be, and say, in Your name. Amen.

Day 22
Obedience because of Deliverance

Read Joshua 22:1–5; Romans 6:17–18

"All this time and right down to this very day you have not abandoned your brothers; you've shouldered the task laid on you by GOD, your God. And now GOD, your God, has given rest to your brothers just as he promised them."

JOSHUA 22:3–4 MSG

- What do you feel you may have left behind so that you could focus more on what God has been calling you to do? What is/was your reward for faithfully following as commanded?

- God wants you to love and serve Him with all your heart and soul. How does your doing so help you with obeying His commands and gaining an unwavering grip on Him?

What does God require of you? To "love GOD, your God, walk in all his ways, do what he's commanded, embrace him, serve him with everything you are and have" (Joshua 22:5 MSG).

What's the result when you do so? Rest. Peace of mind. Because when you obey God, certain other things begin to happen, to slide into place. He comes to your rescue. He delivers you from whatever comes against you. He acts like a hedge of protection around you. He surrounds you with a bevy of angels so that you won't trip up when a stone appears on your path. He will help you to move mountainous obstacles with just a few words. And those things result in rest. Peace. Calm within Him while amid a storm of chaos. What more could a woman of God want?

When you do what God calls you to do, when you're walking the path He has put before you and checked out before you, you are in the best place possible. As Warren Wiersbe says, "The safest place in all the world is in the will of God." And where you feel safe and secure is where you will get your best rest.

Lord, I love You with all my heart and soul. Help me to walk in Your ways, do as You direct, embrace Your presence, and serve You with all I am and have. Amen.

Day 23
Obedience to the One Who Sustains

Read John 15:1–17

Dwell in Me, and I will dwell in you. [Live in Me, and I will live in you.] Just as no branch can bear fruit of itself without abiding in (being vitally united to) the vine, neither can you bear fruit unless you abide in Me.

JOHN 15:4 AMPC

- When you abide in Jesus the Vine, His sap flows through you, energizing, nourishing, and loving you. What steps do you take daily to keep yourself abiding in Jesus?

- How does obedience become a natural thing to one who abides in Jesus the Vine, tended by God the Gardener? How much easier to bear fruit, to ask and receive?

- Jesus chose you, to live in, love, and save you. How does that knowledge make it easy for you to love Him and others in return?

What does it mean to abide in Jesus? To connect with Him on every level, every plane, every part of you? That means spending some quality time in His presence. As you do so, you will become more familiar with His nudges, His whispers,

His rhythm, His grace. You will become aligned with His wants, desires, choices, and directions. All day, every day.

Imagine being so close to Jesus that you, living out His Word and ways, begin to automatically act like Him— putting others before yourself, loving the seemingly unlovable, looking to humble yourself to serve.

That's Jesus' dream. His greatest desire is to see you dwelling in Him. For then He becomes such a part of you that you don't know where He starts and you end.

Jesus became human so that you could be more spiritual, so that you would recognize that there is more to life than just existing, protecting and serving just yourself. Life is about connecting with others, and that begins with connecting with the one who sacrificed all so that you and He could be together forever.

Lord, I open my entire self—body, soul, mind, heart, and spirit—to You. Your touch, Your love. My desire is to be so entwined with You that I know not where You begin and I end. Help me to get there, to dwell so deep within You that You are ever present with me. Amen.

Day 24
Obedience Brings Strength

Read Luke 6:46–49; Acts 4:18–21

*"Why are you so polite with me, always saying 'Yes, sir,'
and 'That's right, sir,' but never doing a thing I tell you?
These words I speak to you are not mere additions to your
life, homeowner improvements to your standard of living.
They are foundation words, words to build a life on."*

<small>LUKE 6:46–47 MSG</small>

- Jesus wants you to come to Him, listen to what He is teaching you, and then *obey* that teaching. How do those three steps shore up your faith?

- In what areas of your life might you be calling Jesus "Lord" but not following through with what He wants you to do?

- When has your faith and obedience given you the strength to do and say what God has called you to do and say, even though it meant going against the crowd or authorities?

Every week you go to church. You greet all the familiar faces, perhaps a visitor or two. Once the service starts, you sing a few Christian songs. Perhaps you're even part of the worship team.

At some point you settle in to listen to the message the presiding minister brings. Chances are you realize you need to make some changes in your life—to love others more, work on your forgiveness skills, perhaps spend more time with God in prayer.

When the service ends, you may fellowship with other attendees and then head home. As the minutes tick by, the music you sang and the message you heard take a back seat to other things happening in your life. And soon you've forgotten all about heeding the message you heard at church or read in your devotions. You may have forgotten about all your good intentions to follow God more closely, obey and serve Him better.

Then something happens at work or at home or school. And your life begins to crumble. You feel like the woman who built her house on sand. The storms have come, and your house has crumbled or floated away.

Jesus wants you to wake up. To look up. To build your life on His words and wisdom, not your thoughts and insights. Perhaps today is the day you shore up your foundation of faith.

Lord, help me shore up my life by obeying
Your words and ways, not my own.

Day 25
Obedience to Truth

Read Psalm 1; Acts 5:28–32

How well God must like you—you don't walk in the ruts of those blind-as-bats, you don't stand with the good-for-nothings, you don't take your seat among the know-it-alls. Instead you thrill to GOD's Word, you chew on Scripture day and night.

PSALM 1:1–2 MSG

- God's Word holds gems of wisdom that can help direct you and your life. What would happen if you made it your daily intent to look with delight for such treasures of truth? What jewel have you found today?

- How does meditating on the truth of God's Word and then *obeying* it not only nourish but prosper you in your life?

- How does knowing you have the Holy Spirit, the harbinger of all truth, living within you make you more confident?

When you live your life knowing and obeying God's truths, you delight your supernatural and all-powerful Creator. You are like "a tree replanted in Eden, bearing fresh fruit every month, never dropping a leaf, always in blossom" (Psalm 1:3 MSG).

Perhaps you don't feel as if you're blossoming or bearing any fruit. If so, you need to get back into God's Word. To spend time amid its wisdom. To read a passage or chapter until something strikes you deep within. To chew on those verses that are speaking to your heart, meditating on them, writing them down, memorizing them, allowing them to feed that spiritual craving deep within you. And then you need to obey what those words, those verses are making clear to you, making them a part of your life. When you do, the Lord will watch over your path. He'll make sure you stay on track. He will chart the road you take where you will not only find the joy of the Lord but prosper as you walk with Him.

Lord of my life, give me a craving for Your good Word. Guide me to the passages I need to read then write upon my heart and mind. Show me the way You would have me go so that I will be on the path You've designed just for me.

Day 26

Obedience without Question

Read Genesis 12:1–4; Deuteronomy 11:1–15

The LORD had said to Abram, "Leave your native country, your relatives, and your father's family, and go to the land that I will show you."... So Abram departed as the LORD had instructed.

GENESIS 12:1, 4 NLT

- Abram stepped out in faith, obeying without question, not knowing where he was headed. When have you done the same? How did God bless your obedience? What miracles did He perform?

- Where might God be calling you to step out now? What armies or obstacles may be keeping you from walking out in faith?

- How does it feel knowing that, even though you may for some time wander in a wilderness, God will take care of you because you obeyed without question?

Imagine being seventy-five years old, well settled in mind and ways. Then God comes and tells you to leave all you know—the people who speak your language, your relatives, your father's house, and the land that has nurtured you, the place you know like the back of your hand—and go to some other place. A place you don't know anything about—neither the flora, nor the fauna, nor the inhabitants.

You have no idea how to get there, what you'll find there, where you'll live nor how. But God has said that He'll show you the way. That once there you will be blessed and made a great nation. That He'll bless you and make you a blessing to others.

What would you do?

Abram believed what God told him, what He promised. So he went. He obeyed. He asked no questions, put up no resistance. He simply packed a bag and left "as the LORD had instructed."

The result? Because Abram obeyed God, followed His command immediately and to the letter—without asking questions like "Who will be there? What will it be like? When will I get there? Where will I be going exactly? Why can't I stay here? How is this going to work?"—all that God had promised him was fulfilled.

That's how this works. God says and you do. So how about it? Are you ready to believe in God's promises and be blessed?

Lord, I believe. I'm ready to follow You—without question.

Day 27
Obedience Yields Blessings

Read Leviticus 26:1–13;
Psalm 119:56–62; James 2:10–13

*LORD, you are mine! I promise to obey your words!
With all my heart I want your blessings. Be
merciful as you promised. I pondered the direction
of my life, and I turned to follow your laws. I will
hurry, without delay, to obey your commands.*

PSALM 119:57–60 NLT

- Your worship of God alone and your obedience to His will and way lead to blessings. How has this been proven in your life?

- Think about where you have been walking lately. What detours have you made from God's path? Where do you need to turn to get back on the right track, following the route God would have you take?

- What disobedience to God might be causing you to trip up completely?

In Leviticus, God tells His people exactly what they can expect when they obey His commands. Their harvest will be great. They'll eat their fill and live in safety in their land.

They'll have peace and be able to sleep at night. They'll be victorious against whoever comes against them. God promises to multiply their numbers, give them surplus crops. He'll even walk among them!

Those same blessings still apply to God's people today! That's why you, along with the psalmist, should obey God's words, expecting Him to stay true to His promises.

Perhaps today you, like the author of Psalm 119, should ponder the direction of your life. Have you walked out of the will of God? Have you made a few detours from the route He's laid out for you? Do you need to turn to follow His wisdom so you can get back on track?

Remember, God knows your beginning and your end. He knows what's best for you, just as any good parent does. At the same time, He wants only good for you. His aim is to bless those who follow Him, who walk His way. So what are you waiting for? Which way will you walk—today and every day—with Him?

Turn my feet to the path You want me to tread, Lord. I want to be following Your path for me, knowing Your blessings await with every step!

Day 28
Obedience Matters

Read Ezekiel 5:7–8; John 14:12–24

*"If you love me, obey my commandments. And I will
ask the Father, and he will give you another Advocate,
who will never leave you. . . . Those who accept my
commandments and obey them are the ones who love me.
And because they love me, my Father will love them. And
I will love them and reveal myself to each of them."*

John 14:15–16, 21 NLT

- When has your disobedience to God resulted in less-than-pleasant circumstances in your life?

- If you are feeling dissonance between yourself and God, take some time to reflect. What might God have been asking you to do or say, or where might He have been asking you to go?

- You show your love to Jesus by following His words and teachings. How does the Holy Spirit help you to do so?

Jesus couldn't have made it any clearer. Or simpler. All who truly love Him, says He, are the ones who obey His words. And for those people, He promises to ask God the Father to send an Advocate, the Holy Spirit, who will be constantly with them and help them live the life they were created to live.

Yet that's not all. Jesus says that all who truly love Him—obeying Him in mind, heart, voice, and action—will be loved by God the Father. And Jesus will reveal Himself to them! "I will let Myself be clearly seen by him and make Myself real to him" (John 14:21 AMPC).

If you're experiencing uneasiness in your physical and spiritual life, spend some time thinking about where you and Jesus or God the Father may be out of step with each other. In this, as in all other areas of your life, ask the Holy Spirit to make clear where you may have taken a detour or have stood still when God wanted you to move forward, left, or right.

I love You, Lord Jesus. Manifest Yourself to me today.
Speak to me through Your Word. Open my eyes
and, if need be, adjust my thinking so I can stay
on the path You would have me take.

Day 29

Growth through His Promises

Read Jeremiah 11:3–5; 2 Peter 1:3–8

*By his divine power, God has given us everything we need
for living a godly life. We have received all of this by coming
to know him, the one who called us to himself by means of
his marvelous glory and excellence. And because of his glory
and excellence, he has given us great and precious promises.*

2 PETER 1:3–4 NLT

- God urges you to, in faith, obey Him, listening to Him, doing all He asks. When you do, He then performs His promises. What are you hearing God speak into your life today? What are you obeying—or disobeying? What promises is He coming through on?

- In what ways do God's promises grow you up in faith, helping you to turn your back on the less-than-perfect world and drawing you closer to the wonders of a life with God?

Your God is a giving God. He has provided you with everything you need to live the godly life. He has provided you with the knowledge of Him by presenting Jesus to you, the Christ that is God in the flesh! And this Christ has called you to follow Him to that eternal glory and partake of His precious promises!

That's a lot to give—and a lot to take in. Yet all we really need to remember is that God has provided us with a pathway to a truly wonderful life in Him. And with that pathway our provision is secure. Thus, we need not stress over the falsehood that we aren't equipped to walk God's way. That we aren't strong enough, good enough, wise enough. We are. We're strong enough because we have the power Jesus promised. We're good enough because female followers are considered by Him to be His precious sisters. And we're wise enough because God's Word helps us to not only take the right path but to stay on it.

With all that help—of Father God, Brother Jesus, and the Holy Spirit—we can stay the course God has set before us, walking strong on the promises He's made, watching them come through one by one by one.

Thank You, Lord, for providing me with all I need to live the life for which You've designed me and for the precious promises You sow along the way!

Day 30

Growth through His Likeness

Read Ephesians 5:1; Philippians 1:27; 1 Peter 1:13–22

Therefore be imitators of God [copy Him and follow His example], as well-beloved children [imitate their father]. . . . [See that you] love one another fervently from a pure heart.

EPHESIANS 5:1; 1 PETER 1:22 AMPC

- God wants you to imitate Him, following in His footsteps, like Father, like daughter. In what ways is His resemblance growing in you?

- What of your old self/life may be trying to call you back into that former world? What of your new self/life is calling you forward, into the world of God? How might you grow your faith to keep you in God's realm?

- How is your love for God, yourself, and others making you more like Christ?

God sent Jesus to not only be a sacrifice for our sins but to also give us an example to follow. We, like Jesus, are to love unstintingly. We are to forgive *everyone*—even those who may persecute us for our faith. We are to serve, not expect to *be* served. We are to give to those in need, minister to those in prison, visit those who are ill, and feed those who are hungry.

Following Jesus' example is not something to just be done on Sundays in church, where people can see you and hear you. It's to be done all day every day. And it's even better when there are no witnesses! For the Lord rewards those who do things in secret.

The more you follow Jesus' example, the more others will be attracted to you. They will want the peace you have when you get cut off in traffic. They will want the hope you have when enduring climate change or a seemingly never-ending pandemic.

When you are new in Jesus, you can't help but shine a little brighter, love a little better, and be a little calmer. Who wouldn't want that?

*Lord, help me every day to become more and more like
You in mind, body, spirit, soul, and heart. Amen.*

Encouragement for Every (Busy) Day!

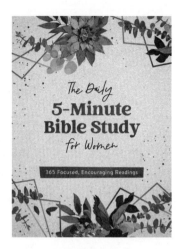

The Daily 5-Minute Bible Study for Women

In just 5 minutes, you will *Read* (minute 1–2), *Understand* (minute 3), *Apply* (minute 4), and *Pray* (minute 5) God's Word through meaningful, focused Bible study. *The Daily 5-Minute Bible Study for Women* includes 365 Bible studies that will speak to your heart in a powerful way.

Flexible Casebound / 978-1-63609-126-6